A SURGICAL ARTIST AT WAR

The Paintings and Sketches of Sir Charles Bell 1809–1815

A SURGICAL ARTIST AT WAR

The Paintings and Sketches of Sir Charles Bell 1809–1815

M. K. H. Crumplin FRCS (Ed and Eng) FINS Hon Cons Surgeon and Hon Curator of Instruments Royal College of Surgeons of England
Captain P. H. Starling (Retd) Curator Army Medical Services Museum

'The value of these acquisitions to the Army Medical School, whether regarded simply as works of art, or in their relations to the history of military surgical science and practice, or as souvenirs of the handiwork of the distinguished author of the *Anatomy of Expression*, can hardly be over-estimated.'

Deputy Inspector-General T. Longmore, CB,
Professor of Military Surgery (1865)

The authors are grateful to the Royal College of Surgeons of Edinburgh and the Drummond Foundation, Regimental Headquarters Royal Army Medical Corps for their generous support in the publication of this book.

Published by

The Naval & Military Press Ltd

Unit 5 Riverside, Brambleside
Bellbrook Industrial Estate
Uckfield, East Sussex
TN22 1QQ England

Tel: +44 (0)1825 749494

www.naval-military-press.com
www.nmarchive.com

Contents

Cover images taken from W. Mudford *An Historical Account of the Campaign in the Netherlands (1817).*

About the Authors

Pete Starling

Pete Starling is a retired Medical Support Officer who served for a total of thirty years in the RAMC. Since first joining the army in 1964, he has had a passion for the history of the Army Medical Services which culminated in his appointment as Museum Curator on his retirement from the army in 1994. During his time as Curator, he has taken the museum through a major re-development incorporating four separate collections into one Army Medical Services Museum. His own particular interests are the Crimean War, the Army Medical Services in Hong Kong, the First World War and the awards of the Victoria Cross to medical personnel, all of which he has written about and lectured on. He is presently writing a book entitled *Mistaken Gallantry: The Awards of the Victoria Cross to Medical Personnel*.

Pete is married to Lesley, a nurse, and has three adult children. His hobbies include reading about the history of medicine and DIY. He is also a committee member of two international military history societies.

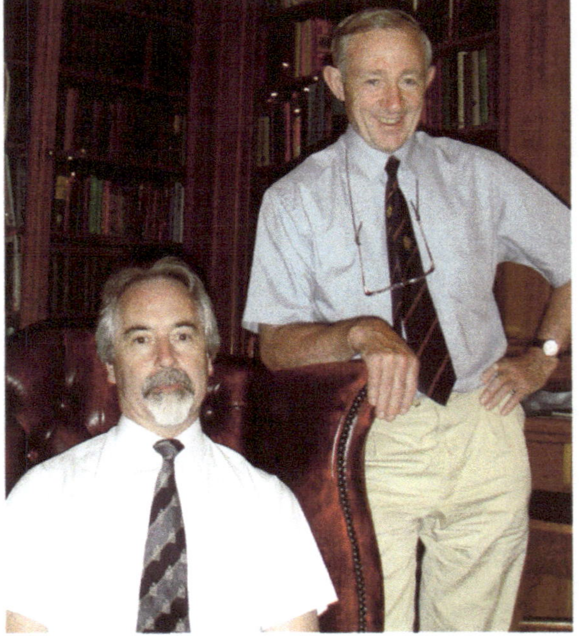

Authors: Pete Starling (seated) and Michael Crumplin

Michael Crumplin

Michael Crumplin is a retired surgeon from north Wales, whose specialties included gastro intestinal, vascular and trauma surgery. Having qualified at the Middlesex Hospital and trained in the south of England, London and Birmingham, he was active in postgraduate education, examining in surgery for the English and Edinburgh College of Surgeons and the Intercollegiate Board of Surgery. He was Chairman of the Court of Examiners of the Royal College of Surgeons of England and served on the editorial board of the *British Journal of Surgery*. He was a council member and is now Archivist to the Association of Surgeons of Great Britain and Ireland.

Having studied medicine during the Napoleonic Wars for forty years, practised widely in surgery and being Honorary Curator of Historic Instruments at the English College, has given him unique opportunities to interpret the philosophy and practice of surgery in these wars.

He has delivered many lectures and demonstrations in Britain and overseas, acted as an advisor for authors and films and has written diverse articles and chapters on various aspects of wounds and their treatment. He is married and has three children.

Foreword

This excellent work highlights the value of clinical observations by a surgeon and recorded by him in oil and watercolour with great skill and sensitivity.

It is difficult for the writer of a foreword not to provide simply a review of the text, which is so tempting in this case. The authors have added a modern commentary to the basic Bell description of each casualty, bringing to life the problems of the nineteenth-century military surgeon who was bereft of our now commonplace and expected investigative procedures and our knowledge of trauma physiology.

Bell has succeeded in achieving not only the pictorial evidence of the wound but also, in many cases, the telling facial expression depicting pain, pallor, toxicity and fear. For some years I was privileged to have copies of four of the Waterloo paintings on the wall of my office in the Ministry, which were admired and envied by all visitors.

Bell is acknowledged as a teacher and organiser rather than a masterful surgical technician when compared to others such as Thomson, Guthrie and Larrey, but his works have left us an irreplaceable legacy and is rightfully displayed in the Playfair Hall of our College.

This book will give immense pleasure to military surgeons and historians as well as background information to all surgeons involved in the management of trauma.

J. T. Coull CB MB FRCS Ed
Major General L/RAMC

The Royal College of Surgeons of Edinburgh is very proud of its collection of the wonderful paintings of Sir Charles Bell. Visitors to the College Museum are always entranced by the subject, the accuracy and the ability to depict the overall effects of war wounds.

Captain P Starling and Mr M Crumplin are to be congratulated not only on drawing together this wonderful collection but also providing a modern commentary. The Royal College of Surgeons of Edinburgh is delighted to endorse and support this publication, which should be of major interest to all surgeons no matter what their specialty or experience may be.

J. A. R. Smith,
President, The Royal College of Surgeons of Edinburgh

500 years
INNOVATION & EXCELLENCE *in* SURGERY

THE ROYAL COLLEGE of SURGEONS EDINBURGH

1505 - 2005

Introduction

Sir Charles Bell

Charles Bell, a Scottish gentleman of lowland stock, was born in Fountainbridge, Edinburgh, in November 1774, the fourth son of the Reverend William Bell and Margaret Morice, herself descended from a line of church ministers. Charles' father died when he was just five years old, leaving Margaret to bring up her sons with very little money. She educated Charles herself and it was from her that he acquired his artistic talent, she having inherited this from her grandfather Bishop White, Primus of Scotland.

Charles, although unhappy with his primary education at the High School of Edinburgh, was one of many illustrious youths from this institution destined for national fame. Sir Walter Scott, Lord Francis Jeffrey and Lord Brougham, to name a few, also attended this school. Margaret Bell had the wisdom to enhance Charles' artistic talents by encouraging an association with the artist David Allan.

Charles elected to follow his distinguished elder brother John into medicine and undertook his studies at Edinburgh University. John Bell was not only a talented anatomist, draughtsman and speaker but also, for twenty years or so, at the turn of the 18th century, he was the leading consultant surgeon in Scotland. Whilst at university, Charles Bell helped his brother in his anatomy school and attended lectures, gaining sufficient knowledge to be trained in anatomy and surgery. For this he owed much not only to John, but also to the teachings of Alexander Monro (*secundus*), a leading professor of anatomy in Edinburgh and the most famous of the three Monros (*primus, secundus* and *tertius*). John Bell taught anatomy and the craft of surgery and was a technical master – none of the three Monros was fundamentally an operative surgeon.

John eventually had to stop teaching anatomy and surgery. Being the most capable technical surgeon in Scotland, there were university and other jealousies. Neither John nor Charles were given operating rights at Edinburgh Infirmary.

In his last year of studies Charles wrote *A System of Dissections Explaining the Anatomy of the Human Body* (1798), which he illustrated with his own drawings. Charles graduated in 1799, and in the same year was elected to the College of Surgeons of Edinburgh, becoming a surgical attendant at Edinburgh Infirmary. He made sincere offers of help to the Faculty of Medicine, offering anatomy specimens, money (100 guineas) and wax models in return for being allowed to draw instructive cases from autopsies. His offer was refused and he was denied these privileges. We have to wonder whether the whole Bell family were not in favour with the university.

Charles' artistic talent and his association with his brother did not diminish after graduation. In 1802 he published a series of engravings of the brain and nervous system to accompany his brother's lectures. Two years later he and John jointly published *Anatomy of the Human Body* (1804). That same year, seeking further advancement, Charles left Edinburgh and arrived in London on 28 November aged 30 years old.

His offers of help to the Faculty of Medicine and his body of published works had brought him to the attention of many eminent London doctors, such as Astley Cooper, John Abernethy and James Wilson (successor to Matthew Baillie, Cumberland Cruikshank and William Hunter in the Great Windmill Street School of Anatomy). Before long he was accepted into their social scene, but this still did not bring him immediate employment.

He was taken under the wing of William Lynn, surgeon to the Westminster Hospital. In his first year in London he completed the plates for his *Essays on the Anatomy of Expression in Painting*. Eventually, in 1805, the year of the Battle of Trafalgar (Nelson's great victory and death) and that of Austerlitz (Napoleon's victory over the coalition), he settled down in Leicester Street and began lecturing on anatomy and surgery to his external and house pupils and anatomy to artists. In 1807 he wrote the first volume of his *System of Operative Surgery*. He had made a reasonable income by 1810, but his expenses were considerable. He was helped financially at times by his other brother and great friend, George Bell.

Mention of the wars against Napoleon in the early nineteenth century recalls the Peninsular War – Wellington's great contribution to the overthrow of Bonaparte. Recalling the triumphs of Salamanca, Vitoria and the Nivelle, we must also remember the great retreat of the British army under Sir John Moore to Corunna in early 1809. This proved to be the salvation of the army.

A British force under Sir John Moore and Sir David Baird were to join up with Spanish forces to rid Spain of the French army. Bonaparte decided to stabilise the situation in Spain and, on the only occasion he personally fought in the Iberian peninsular, he led a large army into Spain. Threatened by a massive superiority of men and arms and unsupported by Cuesta, the Spanish commander Moore began a retreat late in December 1808. He sent the light division to the port of Vigo and his main force crossed the Galician mountains.

After marching almost 300 miles in eighteen days, in unimaginable weather conditions, ill-clad, starving, disease-ridden and harried by the enemy, the allied armies entered Corunna on 11 January 1809. It would be 17 January before the army was able to embark for England, having held and then defeated the French at the gates of Corunna. In doing so, they lost Sir John, one of Britain's most able commanders.

Six thousand men were killed, died of their injuries or were taken prisoner during the march. The tattered army returned to Britain to fight another day. Of the surviving 28,000 men, between 5,000 and 6,000 were sick or wounded. Many had been infected with typhus fever, picked

The Burial of Sir John Moore after Corunna
Charles Wolfe

NOT a drum was heard, not a funeral note,
As his corse to the rampart we hurried;
Not a soldier discharged his farewell shot
O'er the grave where our hero we buried.

We buried him darkly at dead of night,
The sods with our bayonets turning,
By the struggling moonbeam's misty light
And the lanthorn dimly burning.

No useless coffin enclosed his breast,
Not in sheer or in shroud we wound him;
But he lay like a warrior taking his rest
With his martial cloak around him.

Few and short were the prayers we said,
And we spoke not a word of sorrow;
But we steadfastly gazed on the face that was dead,
And we bitterly thought of the morrow,

We thought, as we hollow'd his narrow bed
And smooth'd down his lonely pillow,
That the foe and the stranger would tread o'er his head,
And we far away on the billow!

Lightly they'll talk of the spirit that's gone,
And o'er his cold ashes upbraid him –
But little he'll reck, if they let him sleep on
In the grave where a Briton has laid him.

But half of our heavy task was done
When the clock struck the hour for retiring;
And we heard the distant and random gun
That the foe was sullenly firing.

Slowly and sadly we laid him down,
From the field of his fame fresh and gory;
We carved not a line, and we raised not a stone,
But we left him alone with his glory.

up from the Spanish army at Sahagun and further spread in the damp crowded conditions of the warships and transports. Many of the local Spanish population were so horrified at the sickened skeletons that they crossed themselves in despair. Disembarkation in Britain took place on 20 and 21 January. The towns of Portsmouth and Plymouth were deluged and the sick and wounded men overwhelmed the medical services and hospitals. Medical support was crucial to restoring the vigour of our army. The parsimonious government had dictated that the general hospitals at Gosport, Plymouth and Deal were closed, leaving minimal hospital space ready to receive the casualties. Fortunately, the Portsmouth area had a highly efficient Deputy Inspector of Hospitals for the southwest district in James McGrigor, who later became the paradigm of efficiency as Wellington's Senior Medical Officer in the Peninsula. He quickly set up temporary hospitals in barracks and used hospital ships and hulks to accommodate the sick. The lack of doctors was rectified by sending military surgeons down from London (Household Brigade), medical students and by local civil surgeons volunteering their services.

One of the latter volunteers was Charles Bell. He had regretted not being involved in treating the casualties from Trafalgar in 1805. He was determined not to miss another opportunity to help the British military and set about administering to the wounded.

Of the 2,427 casualties received at Portsmouth, 405 died (a 17 per cent mortality rate).

Bell made sketches of his cases, eventually completing them in oils. These paintings are now in the possession of the Royal College of Surgeons of Edinburgh. Much of his knowledge of gunshot wounds was acquired at this time and was embodied in his work *Dissertation on Gunshot Wounds* (1814).

After his brief experience of the world of military surgery, Bell returned to London and in 1811 married Marion Shaw of Ayr. The couple moved into 34 Soho Square and settled down. Marriage, he found, both suited and stimulated him. He began his experimentation and lectures on the nervous system, especially the cranial nerves. Eventually he discovered that the VII nerve, if damaged, would lead to facial paralysis, what we today know as Bell's palsy. He also had a well-known nerve (supplying the *Latissimus Dorsi* muscle) named after him – the long nerve of Bell.

In 1812 he took over the Great Windmill Street School of Anatomy and in 1814 was appointed consulting surgeon to the Middlesex Hospital. During this time he continued to research and write profusely.

In the summer of 1815 the French and Allied armies met in Belgium, which culminated in the titanic struggle on the fields of Waterloo on 18 June. By day's end there were some 7,000 British wounded to add to the casualties from the previous engagement at Quatre Bras. To this total of over 12,000 must be added the French, Dutch, Belgian, German and Prussian sick and wounded soldiers, bringing the casualty figures to 55,000 in total.

After their initial treatment on the battlefield and in the field hospital at Ferme Mont St Jean, victims made the agonising twelve-mile journey to Brussels. Each of the six large hospitals in Brussels was filled to bursting and local houses were also crowded with casualties. To help ease the burden, carts and canal barges took many of the wounded to Antwerp. Shortage of beds and equipment were not the only problems. There was a dearth of experienced surgeons. Once word of this need filtered back to Britain, several civilian surgeons travelled out to Brussels. Amongst them was Charles Bell, whose only passport was his set of surgical instruments. Having arrived in Brussels on 28 June, he commenced operating up to twelve hours a day until 'my clothes stiff with blood and my arms powerless with the exertion of using my knife'.

Bell took a sketchbook with him and filled it with black lead sketches and scribbled comments on each case.

The original sketches were completed between two and three weeks after the actual injury. The first set of watercolours was completed for teaching purposes when he was appointed to his chairs in London in the 1820s. These have never been found. Also missing was a copy of his *Dissertation on Gunshot Wounds*, which he carried to Brussels and used (on blank interleaved pages) as a notebook for annotations on his cases.

A second series of watercolours, similar to his first series, seventeen in total and life-size, were completed in 1836. These were to complement his lectures on his return to Edinburgh as Professor of Surgery.

Bell went back to his medical duties after his time in Brussels and his work on nerves continued. In 1821 his first paper on the subject was read to the Royal Society. The Frenchman François Magendie would later claim his was the pioneering work on the subject and not Bell's. Bell was already a Fellow of the Royal Society of Edinburgh and in 1826, he was elected a Fellow of the Royal Society. In 1827 he was succeeded at Great Windmill Street by Herbert Mayo (The Middlesex Hospital) and Caesar Hawkins (St George's Hospital).

Appointed as Professor of Anatomy and Surgery of the Royal College of Surgeons in 1824, he was also awarded the chair of Physiology and Surgery at the University of London, but this latter appointment was short-lived and he resigned in 1831 after disagreements with his colleagues. In 1835 Bell was instrumental in the opening of the Middlesex Hospital Medical School. Edinburgh (his alma mater) finally beckoned him back to its bosom and he returned as university Professor of Surgery in 1836. In 1840, on a visit to Paris he was received by Philibert Joseph Roux and Jean-Louis Petit (two influential and talented French surgeons – the latter was the inventor of the well-known screw tourniquet) and displayed to students in Paris. He did not lecture or teach. He was just presented to the audience with the words 'Sharley [sic] Bell, C'est lui-même.'[2] Such an introduction surely a balm to any spirit! He continued to travel south to England regularly and it was on such a trip to London in 1842 that he made a short stop at Hallow Park near Worcester. While sketching, he remarked 'This is a sweet spot – here I fain would rest till they come to fetch me away.'[3]

That night (28 April 1842) he died of a heart attack and was buried in the local churchyard. As long as she was able, Lady Bell made an annual visit to Worcester to visit his grave site.

[2] G. Gordon-Taylor and E. W. Walls, *Sir Charles Bell: His Life and Times*. (Edinburgh: E&S Livingstone Ltd, 1958), p. 159.

[3] Ibid, p. 169.

The Corunna (La Coruna) Oil Paintings

Bell made sketches and subsequent oil paintings of the Corunna patients for the instruction of pupils. These oil paintings must have proven to be unforgettable teaching aids and today provide invaluable assistance for research into the philosophy and practice of contemporary military surgery. These evocative portraits are a few of the 'photographs' of the Napoleonic Wars. They are unique and fully deserve the approbation given to them on display in the Playfair Hall of the Royal College of Surgeons of Edinburgh.

Bell's original annotations taken from the paintings are first quoted and then we have added a brief commentary on each wound and its treatment. There are 15 paintings drawn from some of the casualties delivered back in Britain after the retreat of the British army to Corunna and Vigo between 24 December 1808 and 11 January 1809. About 28,000 of the original force of 34,000 landed on the south coast of England. The local population was horrified at the sight of the bedraggled, ragged, starving soldiers, riddled with typhus and dysentery. The soldiers and their units and locations are not identified by Bell. His comments refer purely to the clinical problems.

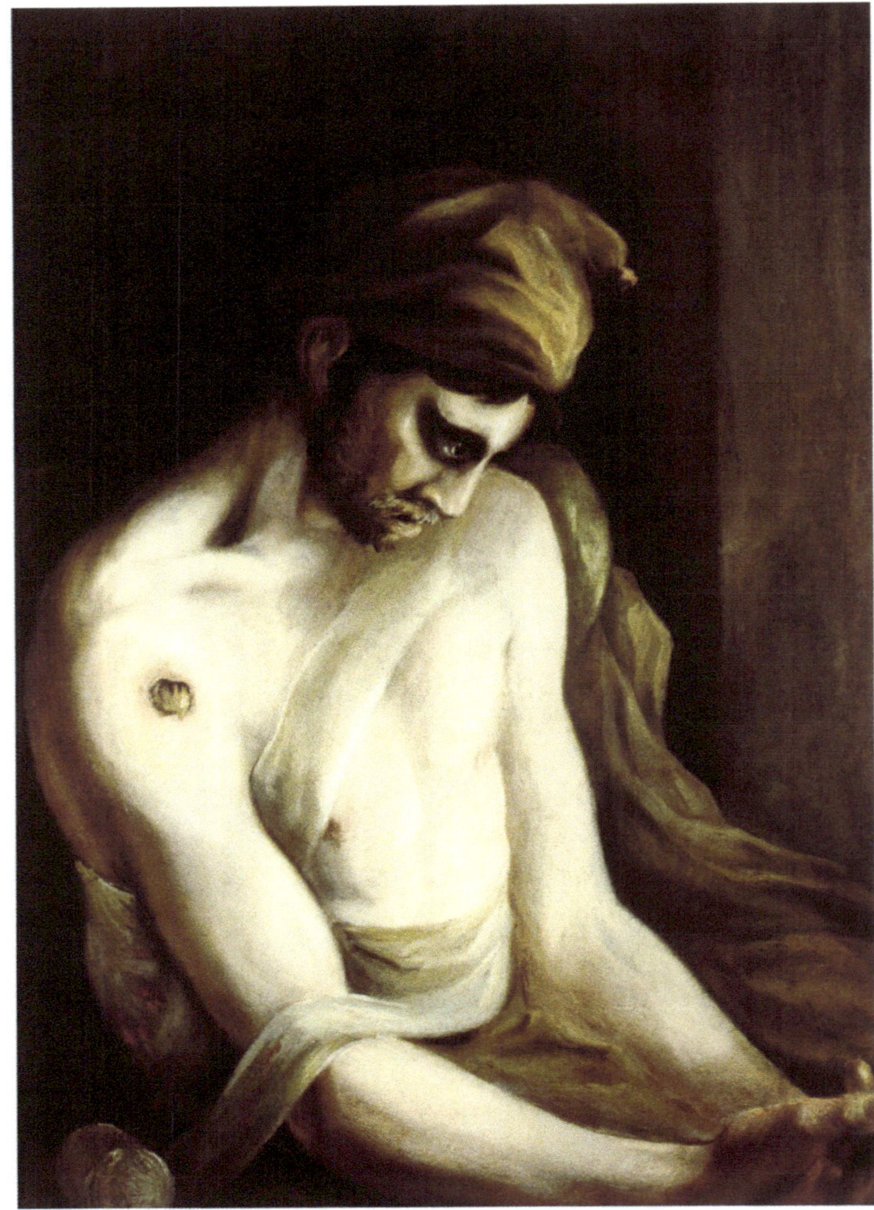

Fig.1 Gunshot wound of the humerus (41.5cm x 51.5cm)

1. Gunshot wound of the humerus (41.5cm x 51.5cm)

This is a sketch in oil of a soldier wounded at Corunna, the ball struck the head of the humerus, and shattered it, passed through and wounded a rib. It was resolved to amputate at the shoulder joint, but the business of the hospital falling into the hands of those from whom I could get little information.

I left Haslar, before the operation was performed. It was reported to me that the patient sunk from the loss of blood, and it was this case that gave rise to my observations on the method of operating. I thought myself entitled to say that the method followed by our army surgeons was too bold, and not suited to common practice, and especially in the case like this, when the patient was reduced by a complication in the wound.

Commentary

Deputy Inspector of Hospitals James McGrigor opened up barracks, prison ships and transports to receive the sick and exhausted men. The Royal Navy offered 1,400 beds in Haslar Hospital, where this patient was treated and may have succumbed. Of the 1,400 sick men accommodated at Haslar, 205 died (14.6 per cent mortality), a higher than average death rate for military general hospitals at that time (roughly 5 per cent overall). Bell was critical of the treatment provided by the army surgeons, perhaps surmising that service surgeons were of an inferior quality and ability when compared with a London (or Edinburgh) trained teacher and city surgeon. To be fair, much military surgical experience had yet to be gained.

Bell's criticisms of the management of this particular case would have been twofold. First, poor vascular control allowing excess bleeding and second, operating on a man in no condition for what Bell had previously acknowledged was an 'operation difficult to perform, as well as a severe one, for the sufferer.'

In terms of the first criticism, Bell previously commented in his texts on capital surgery:

'It is of the greatest moment to save blood. A man is severely wounded; the arm lacerated; the bone shattered; and he is very faint and low from the loss of blood and the severity of suffering. Perhaps he is wounded elsewhere; a grape shot may have bruised his side and broken a rib at the same time, that it has shattered the head of the humerus, and bruised the flesh of the shoulder; in this condition an ounce of blood saved is of consequence. I know not how to express myself in regard to those critics who say that the securing the artery is a matter of indifference; for it makes all the difference betwixt this and other cases of amputation.'

Perhaps the surgeons operating on this man temporarily lost control of the axillary artery during the operation.

In the second critical instance, Bell may have been concerned about performing a complex procedure on a man as yet unfit, as he was 'reduced' due to a complication. In this case the complication may have been profound anaemia, as the patient is painted extremely pale. An alternative might have been sepsis and a discharging wound. The area may well have been contaminated, as the ball would have carried bacteria deep into the joint. Mortality from secondary amputation at the shoulder joint was between 30 and 60 per cent.

2. Old standing gunshot fracture of the shaft of the humerus (28.5cm x 34cm)

Sketch in oil of the state of the arm of an officer two years after the gunshot fracture.

When a case like the preceding one is left without proper surgical assistance, necrosis takes place and the arm presents this appearance. First ulcerations, and exfoliations continue to take place as in this gentleman, according to my experience for seven and ten years, and during all that time he is subject to fever and irritation, not only from the wound, but from any occasional cause which deranges the system, so that he drags on a very weary and uncomfortable existence. These two were Corunna cases, and the first that suggested to me, the improper rule upon which our surgeons were proceeding.

Commentary

Here is another critical appraisal by Sir Charles. He may be suggesting that the chronic sepsis could have been avoided by empirical therapy applied vigorously in the first instance. Or he could be implying that this officer should have long since had a disarticulation or trans-humeral amputation

In the first case, probing and excision of the missile, clothing or tissue would probably not have been easy or complete. Intense antiphlogistic (anti-inflammatory) measures such as venesection (lancet, wet cupping or leeches), purgation (calomel, jalap or magnesium sulphate) and emesis (ipecacuanha) would also have been of little benefit.

Bell was more likely aghast at the length of time the man had tolerated chronic sepsis. The painting indicates that the patient clearly was suffering pain, weight loss and a chronic discharging wound. In fairness to the military surgeons, the officer might have refused amputation. Wounds such as this often dragged the men down so much that eventually limb ablation was requested. Above-elbow amputation or possibly disarticulation at the shoulder would have been appropriate in this case. Surgery was typically performed with the patient sitting up and syncope (fainting) was the usual result. Arterial control was maintained by an assistant firmly pressing on the subclavian artery above the collarbone or the surgeon pinching the neurovascular bundle in the armpit between his forefinger and thumb. Crude flaps were fashioned from skin and fat, then the muscle was divided in an inverted conical fashion. This gave some tissue bulk to cover the bone end. The soft tissues were then retracted using a linen, leather or metal retractor, thus enabling the bone to be transected by a capital saw. The flaps were approximated with linen sutures or adhesive tapes. A lint dressing was then applied along the line of the wound. The lint was covered with the centre of a 'Maltese cross' bandage (whose four ends lay along the stump) and a roller bandage was applied firmly around the four strips.

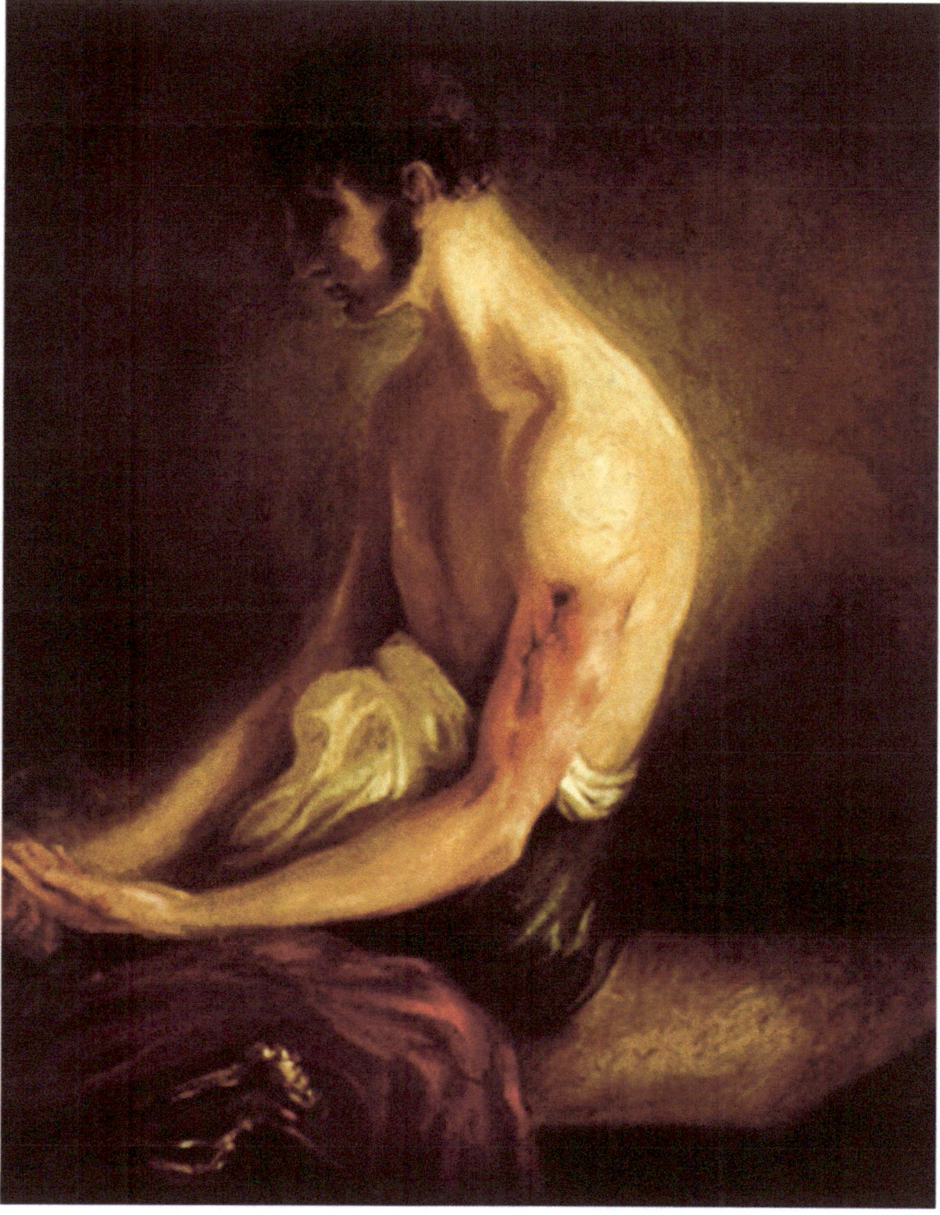

Fig. 2 Old standing gunshot fracture of the shaft of the humerus (28.5cm x 34cm)

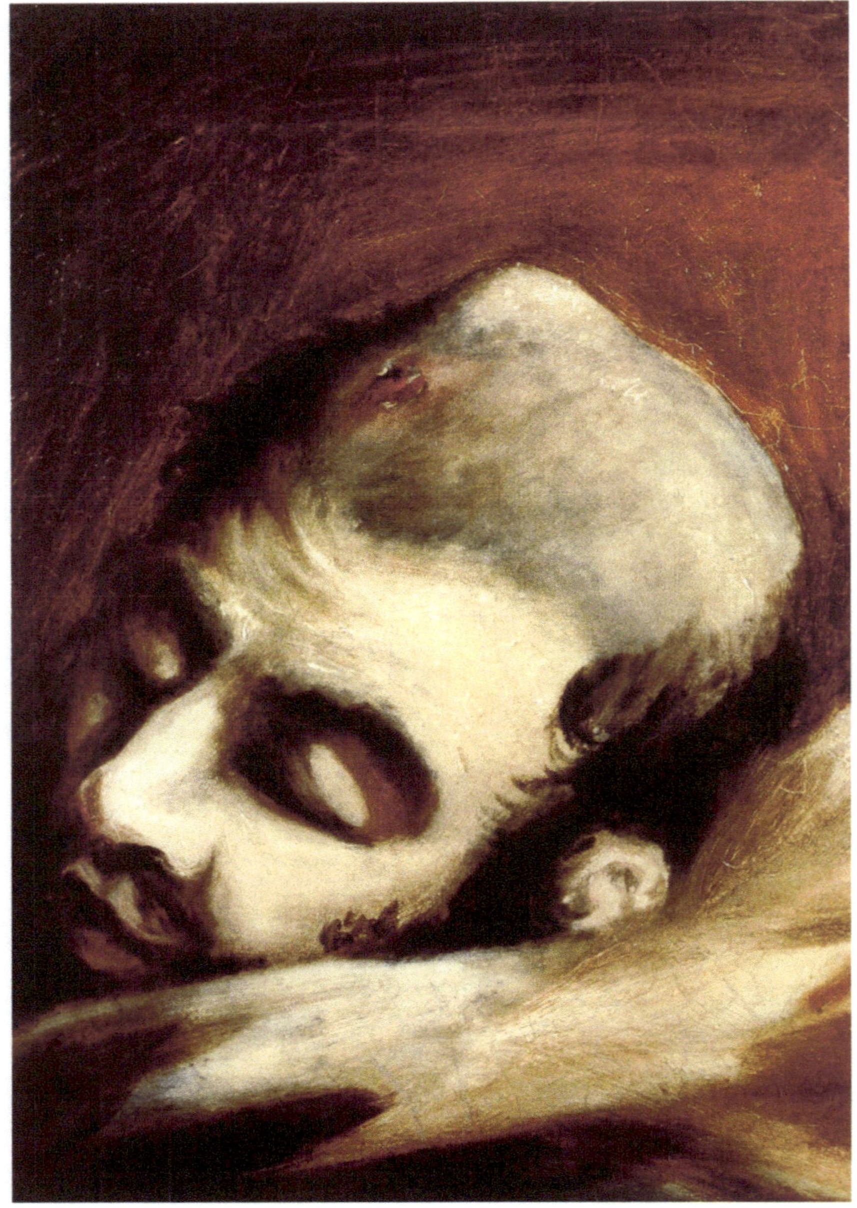

Fig.3 Bullet wound of the skull (28.5cm x 34cm)

3. Bullet wound of the skull (28.5cm x 34cm)

Sketch of soldier, the ball entered in the forehead, penetrated the skull, and drove up the bone, elevating two portions at an angle. The scalp was cut upon at this part, the bone raised, and the ball extracted, as the dura mater was cut, I could expect nothing but fungus cerebri. I lost sight of the man and do not know his fate.

Commentary

The man is pale, languid and clearly very sick. There is an entry wound above the forehead. The ball has tracked under the skull and has struck up two fragments of bone. We cannot clearly see these details as the scalp is intact over the area. There is however a lump on the scalp which we presume, when cut down upon, revealed the two fragments of bone which were deflected up like a ridge tent. The ball was probably resting just under this ridge. A cruciate or longitudinal incision with a scalpel would reveal a bruised scalp and the cranial fracture. The fragments of bone would be removed with bullet or sequestrectomy forceps and the ball extracted. Bell comments on the almost inevitable sepsis caused by the breaching of the dura mater. This is the tough membrane that gives integrity to the brain and is an effective barrier against sepsis. Men did survive with dural damage and brain exposure. This was, however, by no means the usual course.

Bell comments on the likelihood of fungus cerebri, a herniation of the brain, as a consequence of raised intracranial pressure. The raised pressure resulted from the swelling of bruised and infected cerebral tissue. The skull, being rigid, could not accommodate any cerebral swelling. When the brain expanded, it extruded through the hole in the skull and formed a swelling (fungus cerebri). The treatment was excision with a scalpel or bistoury. This was painless and could be repeated. Following this, there would almost certainly be a significant risk of cerebral infection, abscess and epilepsy, should the patient survive. Bell seems justifiably pessimistic about the soldier's unknown outcome.

4. Sketch of a gunshot wound of the thigh (74.5cm x 61.5cm)

Sketch of a gunshot wound of the thigh. It represents the wound in the state of irritation and sloughing, not that sloughing which is a necessary consequence of a gunshot wound, but proceeding from disorder of the system. Twice the arterial blood burst out with a violence that indicated that the main artery opened, and twice the tourniquet was applied with the intention of amputating. See Operative Surgery, *Volume 2nd, page 411.*

Commentary

This is a dangerous wound, carrying a mortality rate following amputation of 60 to 80 per cent in 'average' surgical hands. The wound is soiled with perineal (perianal) bacteria. There is damage to significantly large arteries, either the femoral or profunda femoris vessel or both. There is also sloughing, indicating sepsis and thus further erosion of the arterial wall, with consequent secondary haemorrhage. I suppose what Bell meant by a different sort of sloughing, i.e. not simply that associated with the tissue damage resulting from a gunshot wound, but that proceeding from a 'disorder of the system', was that sepsis that had occurred in the wound. This would cause local pain, swelling, tissue necrosis and liquefaction. There would also be general symptoms and signs of infection. Lethargy, confusion, rigors, fever and wasting would ensue as septicaemia set in.

The soldier's artery had bled twice either as a result of temporary clotting and detachment of the clot and later by erosion of the arterial wall by the 'autodigestive process' of sepsis. Why amputation had not been carried out on either of the two occasions that the tourniquet had been applied must remain conjectural. Either the patient was unfit, a conservative approach had been decided upon, or the pressure of work had been overwhelming. This was a man with significant arterial damage. He could have required an (secondary) above-knee amputation.

Bell refers to his work *Operative Surgery* (Bell's two-volume textbook of surgery published in 1814) in his case description.

What is interesting in the reference given above is that the patient is named and the details of his problem are clarified. The soldier, Rifleman J. Chambers, was in the 95th Regiment and had been shot in the retreat at Villa Franca. Bell relates his story: 'The ball entered under the edge of the sartorius muscle, passed obliquely through the flesh of the thigh and round the bone and lay under the skin near the trochanter major. The wound bled freely on his first receiving the shot. He was thrown on a mule and for three leagues on the retreat he continued to bleed. The surgeon cut out the ball and bound up the limb and then the bleeding stopt [sic]; but it broke out again and continued to bleed for ten days; and after this, when aboard the transport, there was great bleeding [secondary haemorrhage] so that we were obliged to apply the tourniquet &c. The wound continued to bleed till within two days of his coming ashore.' Bell felt that the profunda femoris artery, not the main femoral artery had been injured.

Clearly, this soldier was lucky to survive such continued haemorrhage. His conservative management was unpredictable, but ironically had probably posed less of a threat than amputation.

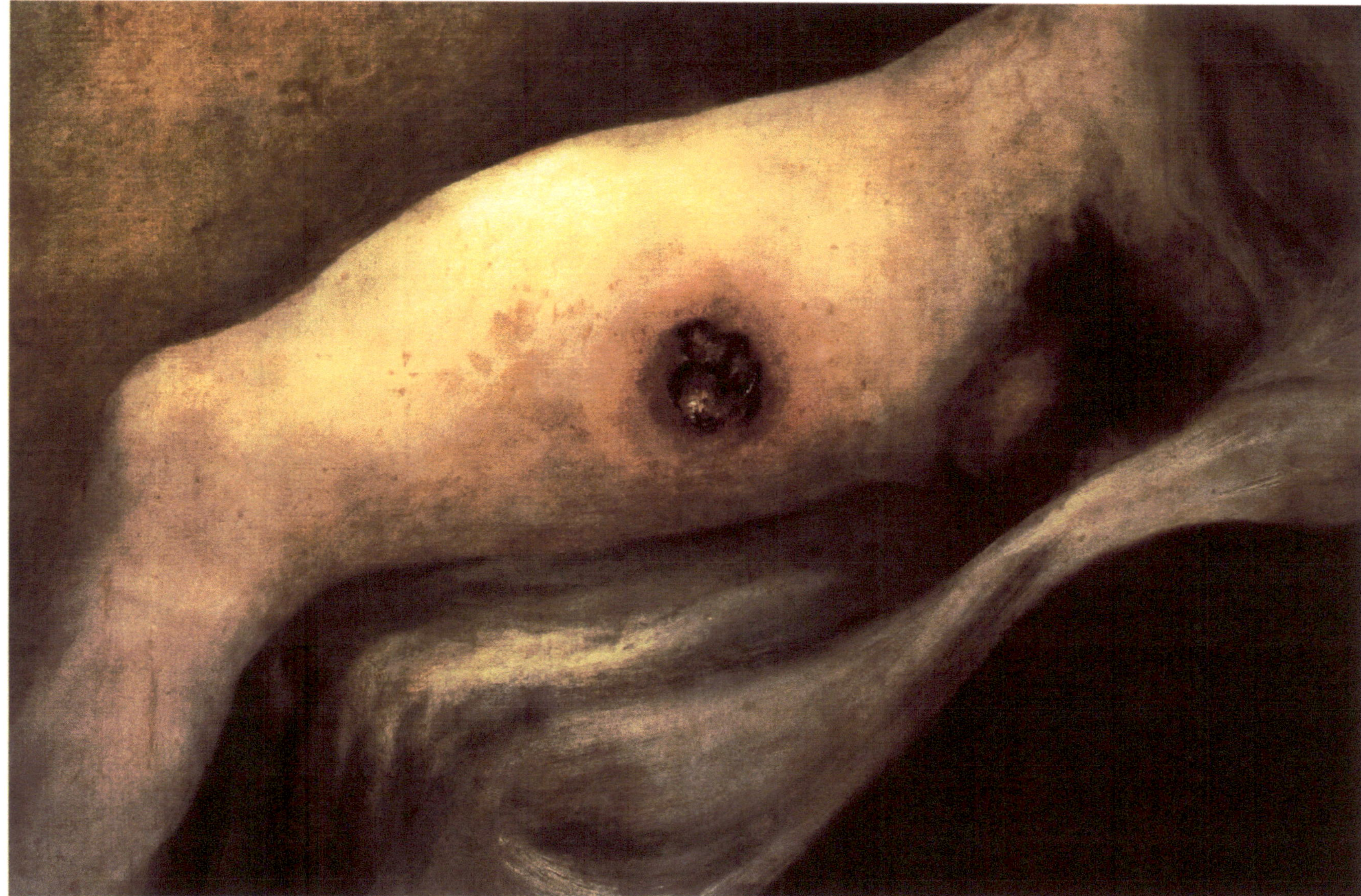

Fig.4 Sketch of a gunshot wound of the thigh (74.5cm x 61.5cm)

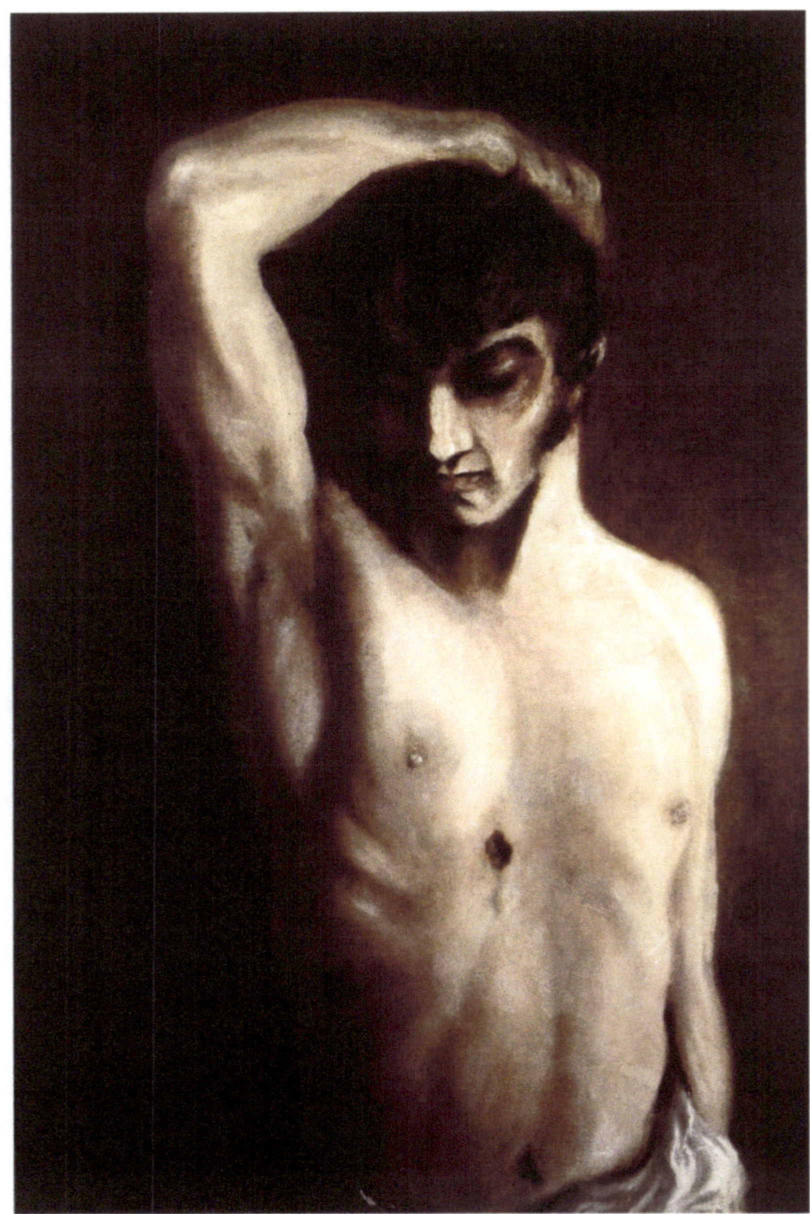

Fig.5 Gunshot entry and exit wounds of chest (61cm x 74cm)

5. Gunshot entry and exit wounds of chest (61cm x 74cm)

Sketch in oil. The ball entered here, on the fore part near the sternum, and it came out near the 7th rib passing through the anterior part of the chest, on the right side, here there was no sloughing, which indicated that the ball had entered the chest, if the ball had passed under the integuments external to the ribs, there would have been more cellular membrane hanging from the wound.

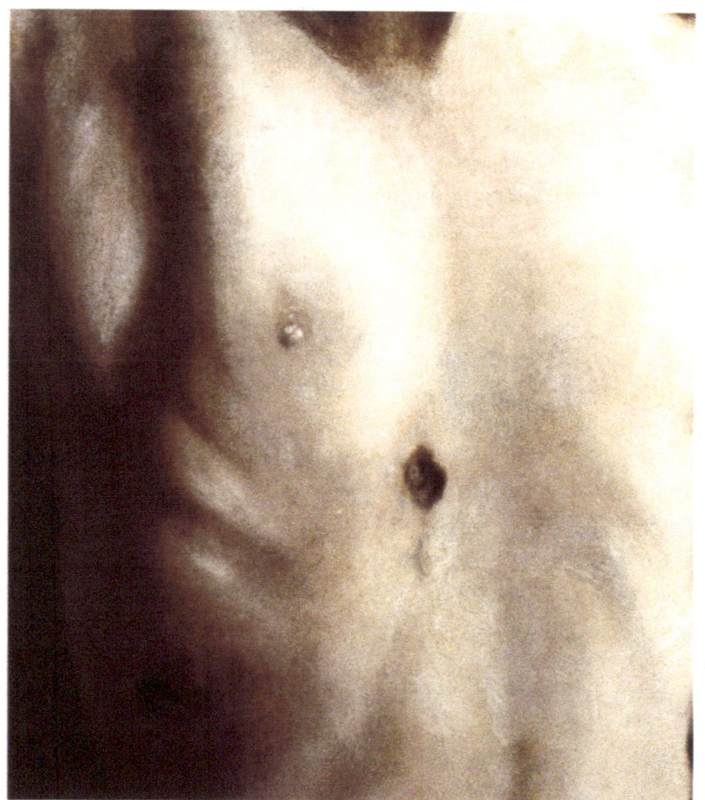

Commentary

In this painting, Bell presents a fairly well-built, fit-looking soldier who has sustained a non-fatal chest injury. The injury is unusual in that there is a tangential passage of the ball through the anterior base of the right chest wall. The entry wound is slightly inflamed and is situated just to the right of the xiphisternum at the junction of the 7th and 8th costal cartilage with the sternum. The ball probably tracked under the 'false ribs' (the costal cartilages), possibly traversing the pleural cavity and causing a pneumothorax. There is significant forensic pathological evidence for this as Bell comments that there is little in the way of protrusion of sloughy 'membrane' from the wounds. This latter was a frequent result of ball tracking through a solid mass of superficial soft tissues. If the ball had gone through the chest cavity for a short distance there would not be a long track of wounded fat and connective tissue. There would therefore be less slough protruding from the wound. This soldier was fortunate to survive. The shot seems to have come from above and to the left of the victim.

I would say, based on the surface anatomy, that the ball exited nearer the 8th and 9th ribs. Presumably the liver has not been injured as there is no mention of bile leak through the wound. This also adds weight to the argument that the wound track is fairly superficial. There are well-consolidated blood clots in the wounds, which have wisely not been stitched together.

6. Old-standing gunshot wound of the fibula (33cm x 28cm)

The leg fell at last into the state of scrophulous joint and was amputated. Sketch in oil of the (above) gunshot wound of the ankle, which degenerated into a scrophulous ulcer.

Commentary

The ball was probably not retained in the wound. There has been a compound fracture of the lower end of the fibula. Infection has caused local swelling and ulceration. This is an unhealthy looking, infected, granulating and ulcerated wound. The ankle joint is swollen and there may well be a septic arthritis. As it was highly unlikely to heal even with local ablative surgery, and because there is discharge and pain, a secondary amputation (below knee) was planned. This would improve the quality of life for the soldier.

The term 'scrophulous' (scrofulous, from the Latin *scrofa*, or a sow – sows were thought to be prone to tuberculous swelling of lymph nodes) is used to describe the wound (ulcer). This would literally mean tuberculous, because the original connotation implied ulcerating tuberculous lymph glands (nodes) in the neck. This resulted from drinking unpasteurised milk and acquiring the infection by the oral route. The term was more loosely used at these times to describe the unhealthy status of a patient or to describe a weeping ulcerated wound such as this.

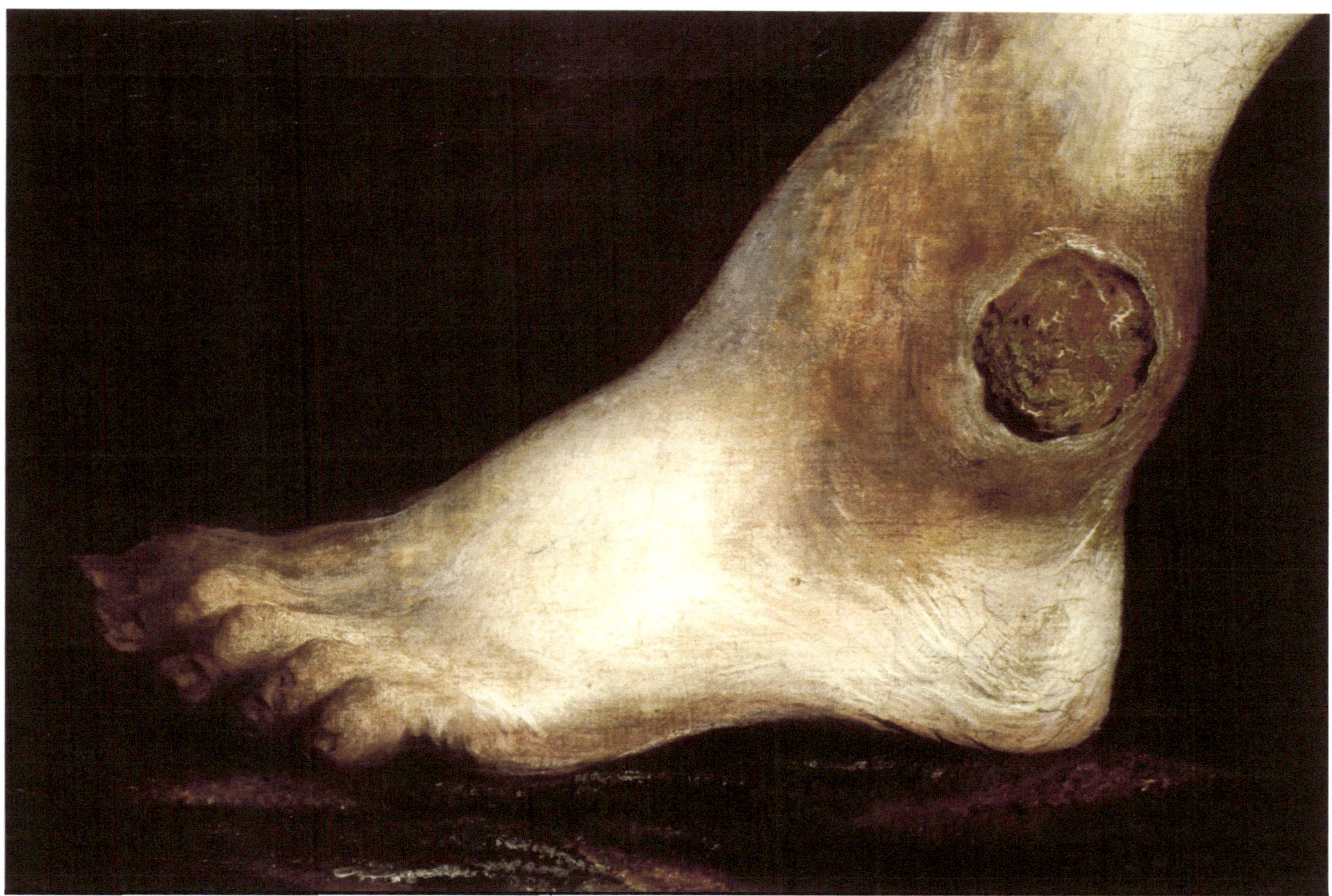

Fig.6 Old-standing gunshot wound of the fibula (33cm x 28cm)

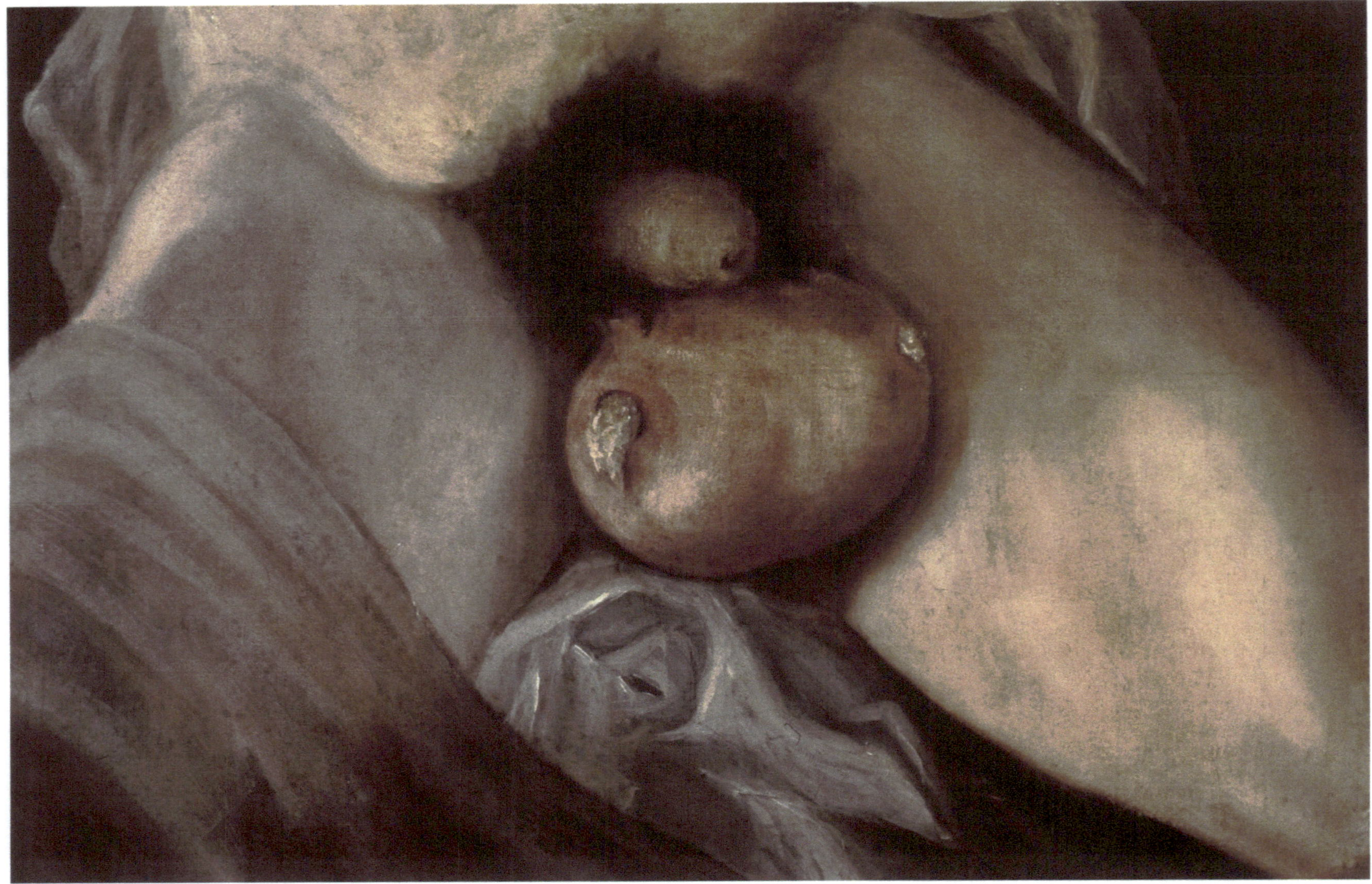

Fig.7 Gunshot wound, testes (48.5cm x 41.5cm)

7. Gunshot wound, testes (48.5cm x 41.5cm)

Sketch of a man wounded in the scrotum, the ball went through both testicles without touching the thighs, even here we may see where the ball entered. There is more inflammation and a larger wound, and a greater quantity of slough hanging from the right side. The sketch was taken to illustrate this fact. See Operative Surgery.

Commentary

Soldiers frequently received this type of wound kneeling to fire or present bayonet. This would usually result in a front to back, through and through ball track across the scrotum. The tracking of this injury is odd, as the scrotum normally hangs back somewhat, between the thighs. The comment by Bell that the ball has not touched the thighs implies that this too has struck him as unusual. The shot must have been received either with the soldier's legs astride or when the scrotum was in a forward position in relation to the thighs.

This is an unpleasant, fairly rare and painful wound which was not without risk from sepsis. The wound is in the vicinity of bowel organisms and dirty, soiled clothing.

The clinical sign, well illustrated by Bell, is the immense swelling of the scrotum. This is the result of a mixture of bruising, inflammation and sepsis. The scrotum has very lax tissues around the testes and any injury (or surgery) is usually attended by gross swelling. Both testes might have been destroyed, causing infertility. Enough testicular tissue would probably survive, however, to preserve some androgen secretion.

Bell comments on the increased amount of slough from the entrance wound, reflecting the track of the ball as it devitalised some of the lax scrotal tissue, which protrudes from the wound. This is necrotic connective tissue and has the characteristic appearance of dead slough. The problem with this is that there is a great deal of this material inside the scrotum. It is a good culture medium for the aerobic and anaerobic bacteria that teem over this area.

One of the unpleasant outcomes here could have been Fournier's Gangrene – a symbiotic bacterial infection of the scrotum that can be rapidly fatal. There is a high chance this soldier would have succumbed from this problem.

Today, the management of this problem (under appropriate antibiotic cover) would be to lay open the scrotum and remove all dead tissue (including the testes if destroyed), control any bleeding and probably pack the scrotum open as there had been so much bacterial contamination. The open wound could be closed later or skin grafted.

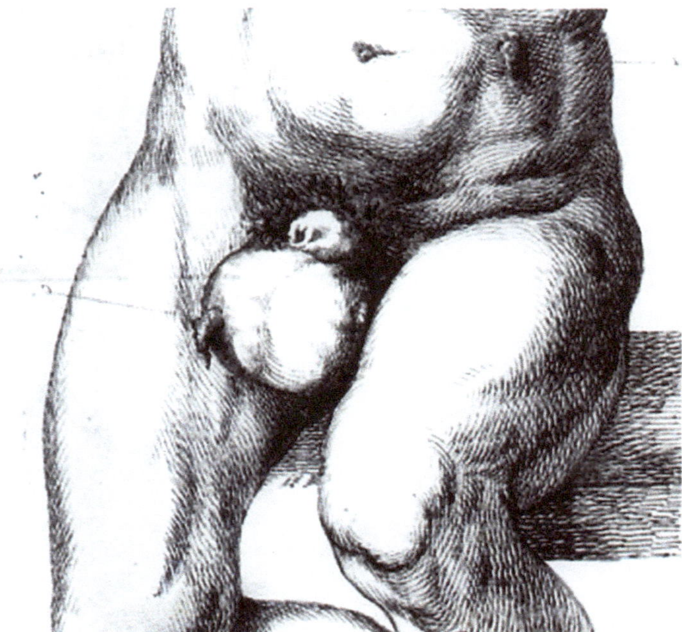

Gunshot wound of the scrotum, drawn by Charles Bell (Plate I vol.1 *A System of Operative Surgery*. London: Longman, Hurst, Rees, Orme & Brown, 1814.

8. Gunshot wound of the head

Sketch of a soldier who received a musket ball in the forehead, which had run under the scalp. I cut it out and found it flattened.

Commentary

This injury was the result of a strike by a spent ball, which entered the frontal region above the left eye. The layers of the scalp consist of thick skin, fat, muscle and areola connective tissue. The muscle is made up of a sheet of fibres, called the occipito-frontalis. The spent ball probably flattened on the bone of the skull and tracked under the muscle. Bell would have pressed on the edges of the scalp to minimise bleeding and made a short cut down onto the ball with a bistoury or common scalpel. The scalp wound would then either have been left open and dressed with lint and a head roller bandage, or possibly stitched with interrupted linen or silk sutures. This wound should have done well. The blood supply of the scalp is notoriously generous.

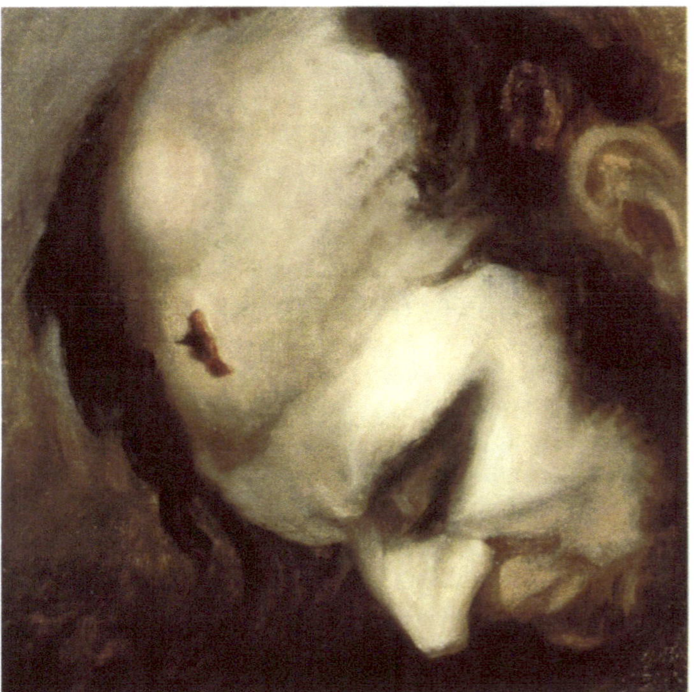

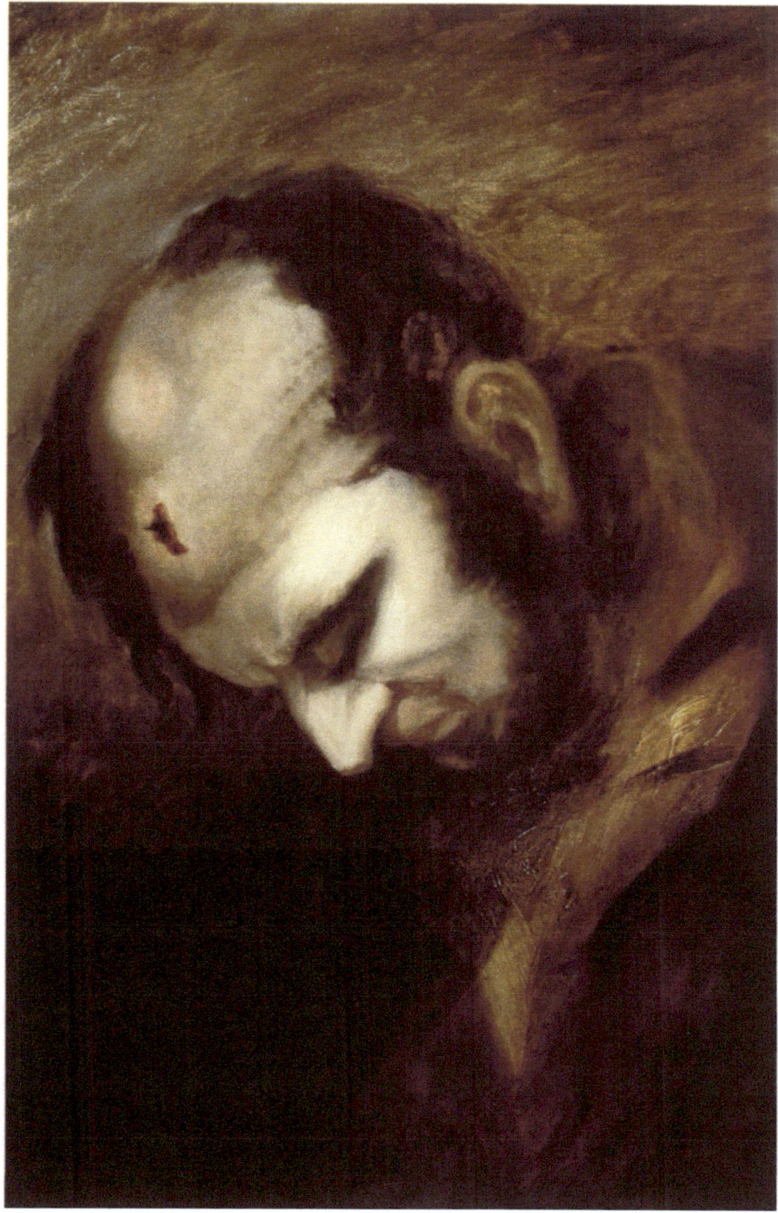

Fig.8 Gunshot wound of the head

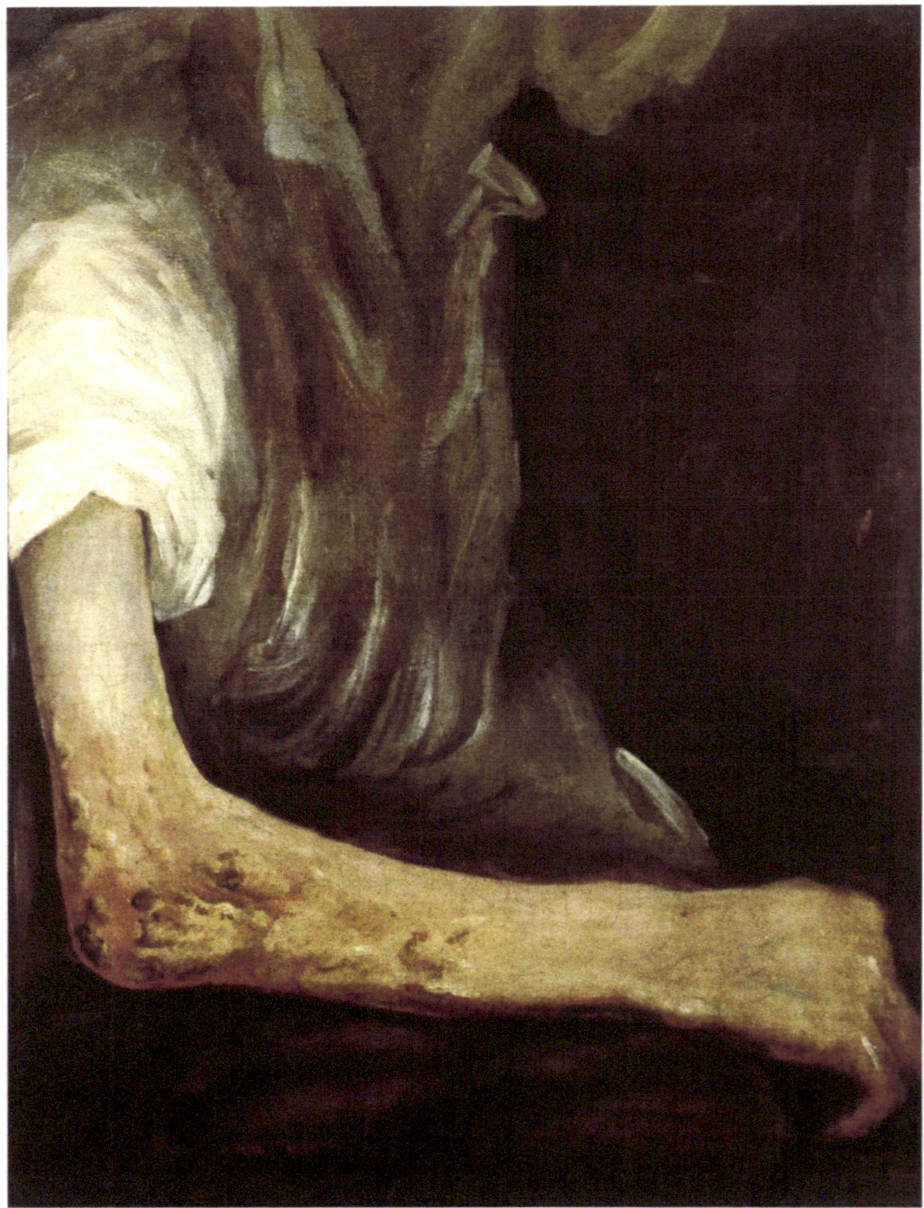

Fig.9 Gunshot wound of elbow (27.5cm x 33cm)

9. Gunshot wound of elbow (27.5cm x 33cm)

Sketch in oil of an arm of an officer who came to me to have his arm amputated. A musket ball is lodged in the elbow joint, the nerves were cut, and the arm asleep, shrunk and cold.

Commentary

Both the right elbow of this officer and indeed the patient himself seem shrivelled and pale. The right arm is grossly wasted and thin. There is a massive reduction of muscle volume of the biceps, brachioradialis and triceps. The elbow is swollen and covered with dried slough. The gross swelling following the compound injury to the elbow has abated and the entry wound is hard to see. It may be that both the median and ulnar nerves were severed and the brachial artery damaged. There may well have been early joint stiffness and ankylosis. The patient is about to undergo a secondary amputation due to the pain and paralysis.

This would be an above elbow excision, with a mortality rate of 15 to 30 per cent. Significant joint injury or sepsis were absolute indications for amputation. Not a few officers would defer surgery in the hope of spontaneous improvement. All the surgeon could do was to await the outcome. The patient here is clearly debilitated and would be better off with ablative surgery.

Sepsis entered the joint via the piece of clothing carried in by the spherical ball. This was a particularly painful injury and healing was always impaired by unhealthy exfoliations (granulations – excessive and poor-quality healing tissue) from the bony and cartilaginous injury.

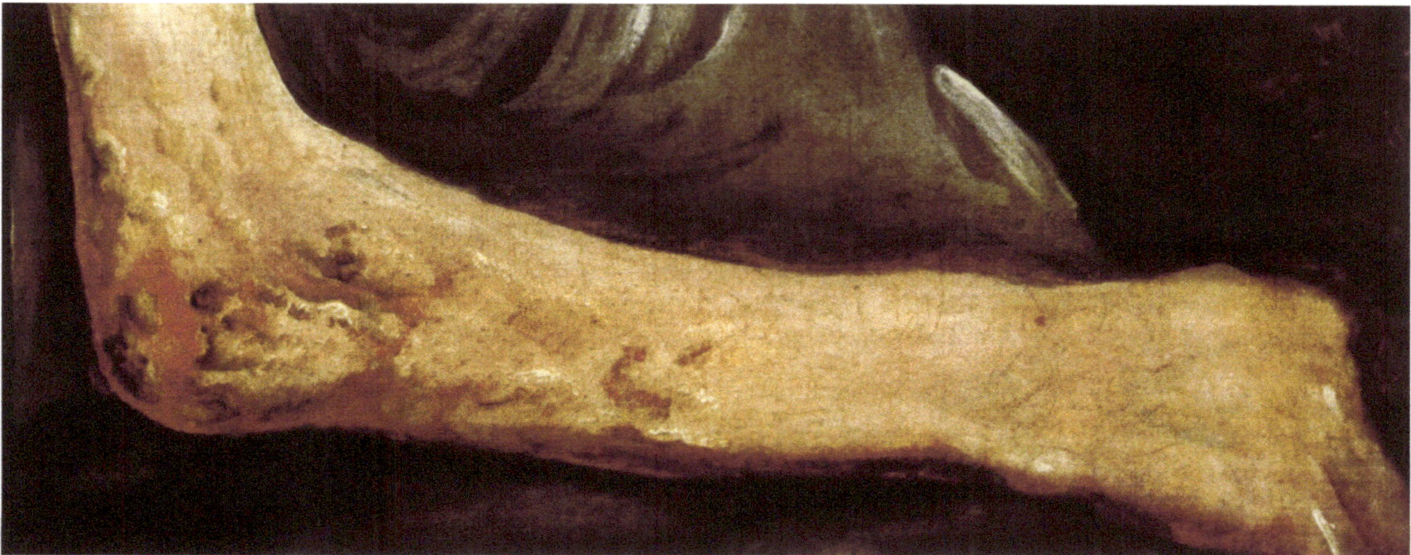

10. Gunshot wound of the clavicle and scapula (35.5cm x 30.5cm)

The musket ball is lodged in the back of the scapula this I took from the body of Capt … The ball entered in the breast, broke the end of the clavicle, entered the chest, and went across the lungs, broke a rib on the back part, stuck in the scapula the spent ball being nearly divided in two by the spine of the scapula; I was present when he was brought ashore in Portsmouth, in a very exhausted condition, and labouring in his breathing, he died the next day, which was the twelfth from receiving the wound. On opening the body I was astonished at finding the quantity of serum, which poured out from the chest, as out of a barrel, the lungs were condensed and gorged with blood, he would have been much relieved by the operation of paracentesis. See Operative Surgery, *2nd Edition in the description of plates IV and XIII.*

Commentary

This officer might have survived with prompt treatment. The corpse was painted with deference to the soldier's identity in death, his face partly concealed by a linen cloth. The fatal ball has entered by breaking the sternal end of the clavicle and has injured the sterno-clavicular joint and probably the first and/or second rib. It smashed across the pleura and lungs then went through the fifth rib behind, ending up in the scapula (shoulder blade). The ball, as not infrequently occurred, was almost split in two by the bony ridge, known as the spine of the scapula.

This soldier lived for twelve days, obviously in great discomfort, with immense and increasing difficulty with breathing. The ball had not only caused the bony damage but had also, in passing through the lung tissue, caused bleeding and partial lung collapse, predominantly of the upper lobe.

The remarkable thing to Bell was the immense amount of 'serum' (straw-coloured fluid) trapped in the chest. Whilst this could be old and altered blood, the slight possibility of damage to the right thoracic lymphatic duct must be considered. This is the delicate tube which carries the lymph from the abdomen and chest into the neck, where it drains into the main venous system. This is the way lymph is carried from the body into the circulation. The duct is situated at the back of the thorax and, as it is inaccessible, is rarely injured by trauma. The turnover of lymph is large and if this duct is damaged, the patient could lose between one and two litres a day through this defect. This might just have accounted for the large volume of fluid accumulated in this officer's chest. The tragedy was that had a surgeon pushed a metal trocar and canula (bronchotomy tube) into the chest (what Bell calls 'paracentesis'), this build-up of fluid could have been, at least temporarily, relieved. However, if there had been a lymphatic leakage this would never have spontaneously ceased to drain. The officer would then have died of starvation (with the gross protein depletion) and fluid loss, as this problem does not tend to resolve itself spontaneously.

Perusal of plates IV (Figure 3) and XIII and their commentaries in the second volume of Bell's *Operative Surgery* reveal only one further pathological comment on the post mortem: 'All the upper part of the lungs of the left [does he mean right?] side, were of a liver-like firmness, from extravasation and inflammation.'

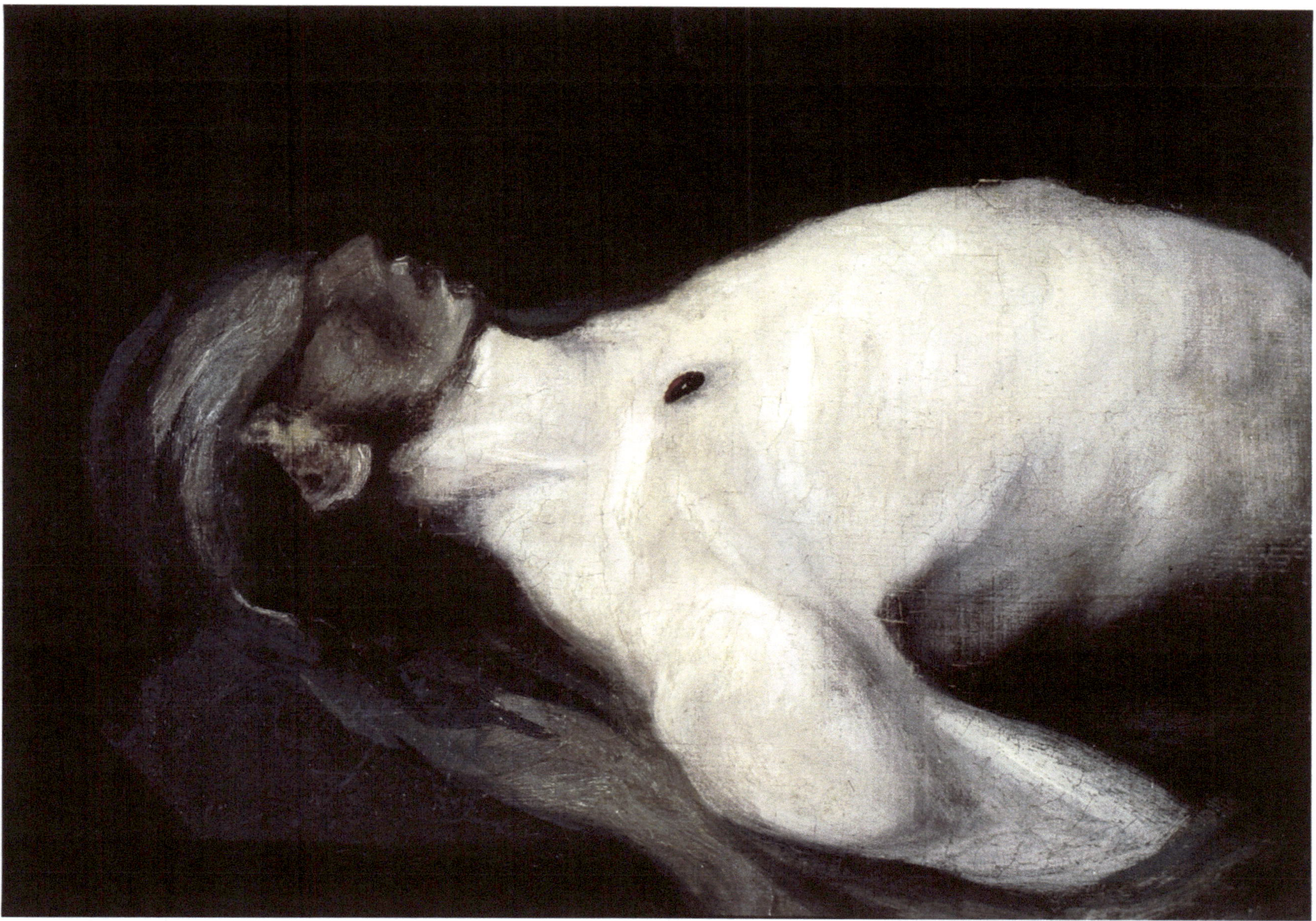

Fig.10 Gunshot wound of the clavicle and scapula (35.5cm x 30.5cm)

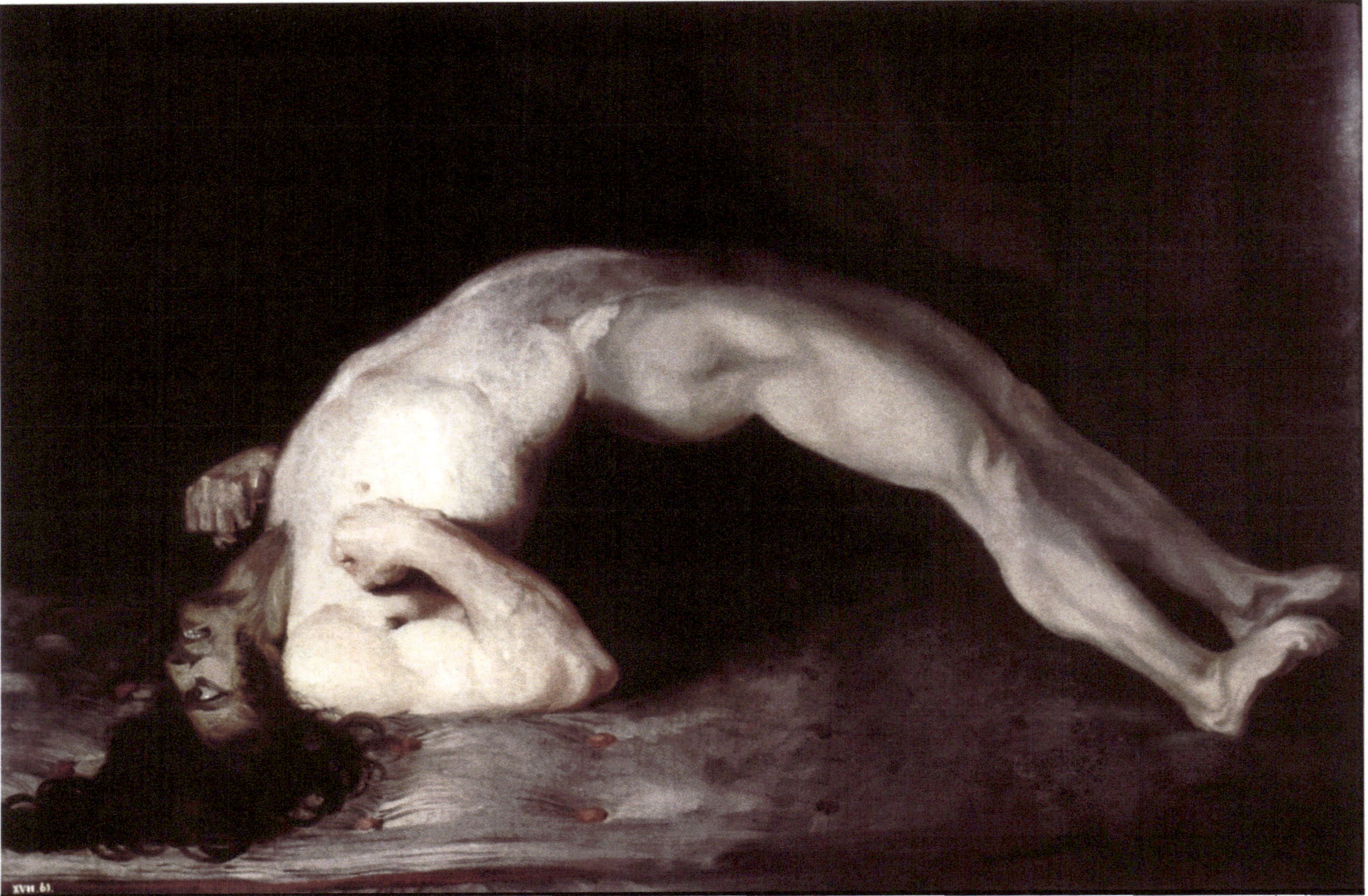

Fig.11 Tetanus following gunshot wounds (90cm x 69.5cm)

11. Tetanus following gunshot wounds (90cm x 69.5cm)

Sketch in oil of opisthotonus taken from three soldiers, who were wounded at Corunna, and brought to Portsmouth. They died successively from gunshot fractures of the skull.

Commentary

This is certainly the most dramatic, if not the most famous, of Bell's paintings. He annotated this illustration scantily, attributing the painting to an amalgam of three individuals who presumably had suffered the same type of wound and infection. The head wound is not visible and the soldier is placed on an expensive mattress to suffer his ghastly illness.

The head injury was probably not life-threatening but it only took minimal inoculation of the bacterium clostridium tetani to convert these men's wounds into full-blown opisthotonic tetanus (tetanus is derived from the Greek 'to stretch').Tetanus was frequently a lethal infection and there were few survivors at this time. Two, however, lived following this problem after the Battle of Waterloo. Voultz, a soldier serving in the King's German Legion (KGL) (see Waterloo painting no. 16) and an unnamed French infantry officer.

Horse manure and farm soil are abundant sources of these clostridia. The first sign of trouble, usually five to fifteen days after inoculation, was a stiffness and mild spasm of the jaw muscles. This was termed trismus (or lockjaw). The neck stiffened up and swallowing was impaired, which made it difficult to keep the patient nourished. Like those with rabies, the patient sometimes became terrified at the sight of water. Tetanic muscular spasms would increase in severity, causing violent contractions of the great muscles of the back. This threw the patient into an arched position, as the painting so graphically shows. The spasms were sudden and painful. Frequently, the tongue was bitten and the patient became exhausted. In between spasms, the patient was relaxed, as normal. Management was by rest, isolation and sedation with opium (5 to 20 grains every two to three hours!) or laudanum. Antispasmodics such as camphor or musk were also used. Occasionally, the doubtful practice of throwing pails of water from several feet up over the unfortunate patient was used as warm baths and fomentations were found to be of little value. In a similar vein, Sir James McGrigor found a guardsman in northern Spain suffering from tetanus after a trivial finger injury. When the soldier went into the high mountains and cold temperatures, his symptoms improved. McGrigor and Guthrie both recommended venesection, catharsis and diaphoretics (to induce perspiration) for the several hundred cases treated in Spain.

Operating was not recommended by the majority of surgeons (incision or amputation) but the cautery was occasionally applied to the wound by some French surgeons. Baron Larrey often extracted two incisor teeth from the patient to enable feeding with a gum-elastic catheter or spoon. If the patient could not take medication by mouth, it could be administered by glyster (enema).

12. Gunshot wound of the humerus (28.5cm x 34cm)

In this sketch in oil the apparently trifling nature of the wound, is represented. Through such a wound however the finger can be introduced, and if the bone be shattered, and in this instance, jagged points of the fragments will be felt, all around. The observation made to me on this very case was to this effect, when I feel the bone broken merely I do not amputate, but when I feel it thus, the finger passing through the bone, this is the case for amputation.

Commentary

This painting is interesting not only because of its clinical content but also as there are some interesting surrounding features painted in. The patient is being examined in either a hospital marquee or a bell tent. There are other tents in the vicinity. This could be a regimental hospital tent. The soldier's scarlet jacket hangs behind him and his wounded arm rests on a table. The pillow supporting his arm lies on what appears to be a clinical case record book. A pair of steel forceps (or lever) also lies beneath the pillow. A small steel pin for a roller bandage sits on the edge of the table.

As far as the injury is concerned, the initial swelling from the gunshot wound has probably settled as far as it will. The man's joints above and below the injury seem satisfactory. There is a sloughy coagulum (scab or eschar) over the compound fracture.

Bell used his finger as his prime diagnostic aid. In the absence of X-rays or adequate operative exposure under anaesthesia, his forefinger gave him the information he required. What Bell rightly says is that in the case of a straightforward fracture, which is not comminuted (many fragments of bone), with no evidence of vascular or nerve damage, but with some sepsis, a trial of conservative management is reasonable. Here the bone is so shattered as to be a target for prolonged and debilitating infection. Chronic pain, discharge and poor health are inevitable. The arm must be removed.

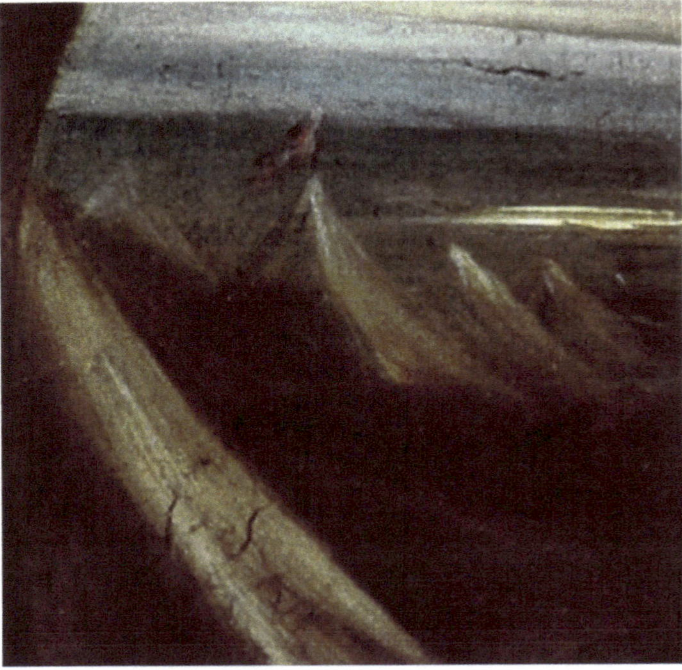

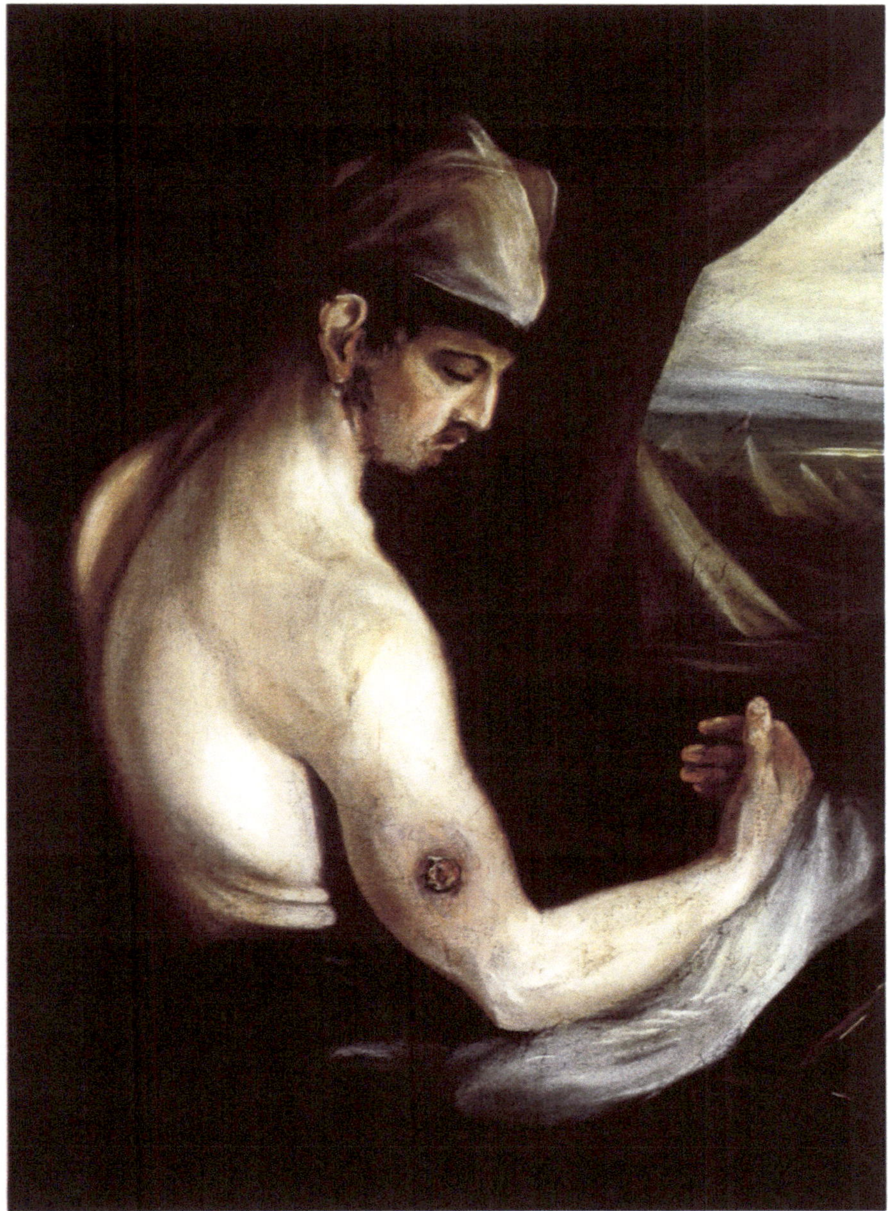

Fig.12 Gunshot wound of the humerus (28.5cm x 34cm)

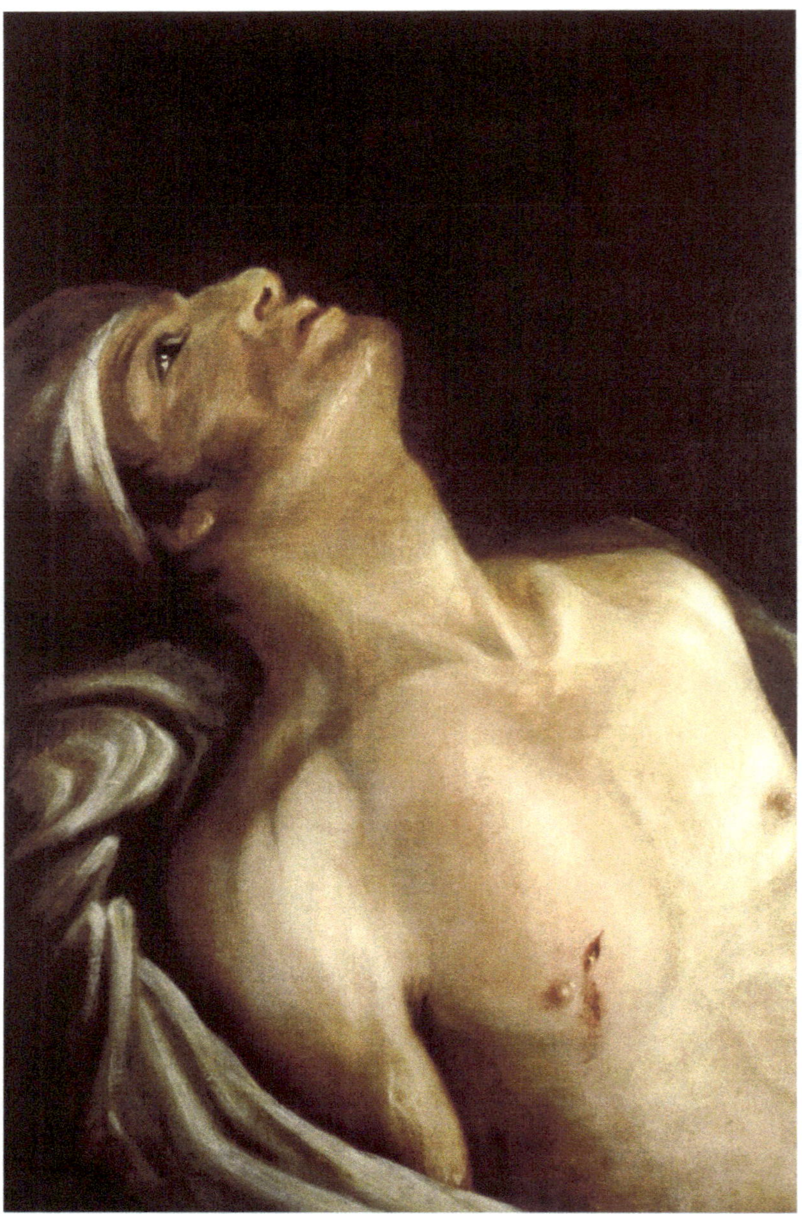

Fig.13 Sketch in oil of a man wounded in the chest (49cm x 58.5cm)

13. Sketch in oil of a man wounded in the chest (49cm x 58.5cm)

Sketch in oil of a man wounded in the chest, the ball entered at the back, an abscess formed on the fore part of the chest. An incision made where it is represented on the fore part disclosed the ball lying in the abscess. This was a man from Corunna, and there lay beside him, in the ward at Haslar, a man wounded in the same place, that is, having a wound on the back part and on the fore part, but the ball had penetrated the chest, and came directly through, whilst in this man the ball passed over the shoulder. This man never had spitting of blood, or any affection of the lungs, the other had bloody expectoration from the moment of receiving the wound.

Commentary

Bell compared two cases here and rightly emphasised the diagnostic features that differentiate the penetrating chest wound from the spent ball injury, which is far less life-threatening. The injury suffered by this man was caused when a part spent ball entered the posterior chest wall. Unusually, it has tracked over the scapula and over the shoulder region in the subcutaneous tissues onto the front of the chest wall, where an abscess has formed. The strange thing is that there is no red swollen track running over the shoulder into the abscess. The probable reason for this was that the tract swelling has abated during the sea voyage and the abscess lying over the pectoralis major muscle developed later.

The patient looks flushed as a result of the sepsis. The abscess was easily treated by a small incision with a bistoury, correctly made in the dependent part of the cavity. Pus was released and the ball was extracted. Today the surgeon would make a slightly larger incision and insert some type of drain for a short while.

The patient would have a good prognosis after this injury and treatment. He is a well-built soldier and would not look this well if the ball had passed through the chest cavity. He did not have haemoptysis (coughing up blood) that the other patient suffered. This latter patient would have had air in the thoracic cavity (pneumothorax) and bled to a greater or lesser degree. Spitting up blood was a result of the ball passing through the spongy lung tissue. The haemorrhage caused some blood to leak into the small airways, which was then expectorated (coughed up).

Clinicians at this time had to rely on simple clinical observations (i.e. inspection, percussion or listening to chest sounds with the ear), as neither the stethoscope (introduced in 1816) or chest X-rays were available.

14. Bullet wound of the skull (33cm x 28cm)

Sketch of a soldier struck on the head by a musket ball, a circular portion of bone was depressed, which upon inspection consisted of minute fractured portions (which are seen in no.7a). [Authors: We are unable to trace this reference]. *This man had no bad symptoms and did well.*

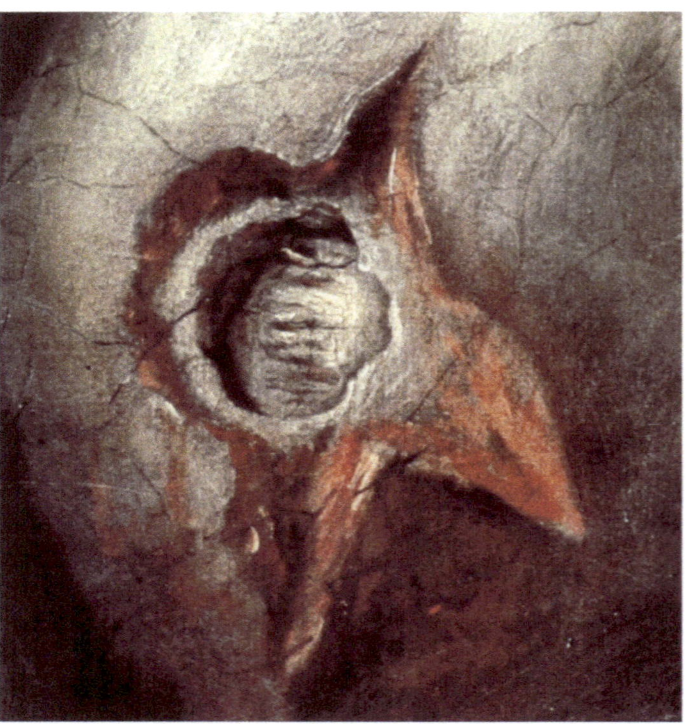

Commentary

There is what appears to be a trephine defect (a circular hole created by the circular trephine saw) in the skull in this picture. On closer inspection, however, the edges, although fairly neat, are rather irregular. Bell reports that there was a circular portion of bone which was depressed and fragmented into small splinters. Typically, the surgeon would trephine next to this defect and elevate or remove the fractured bone pieces.

I suspect that in this case Bell was able to lift out the fragments and tidy up the wound rather than trephine. He may well have 'rounded off' the defect with a sharp-edged lenticular (a side cutting knife with a blunt button end to avoid dural and brain damage when inserted). What we see at the base of the defect is either the detached and depressed bone fragments or the dura mater. The dura mater may well have been lacerated by the fracture. Bell has cut down on the fracture with a trefoil incision. He would have approximated the linear incisions with roller bandages and possibly adhesive straps or occasionally sutures. Cranial defects after trepanning did not close over. The edges of the skull wound merely became smooth.

We can only assume that once again the ball was at least part spent and easily extracted as the wound was fairly superficial.

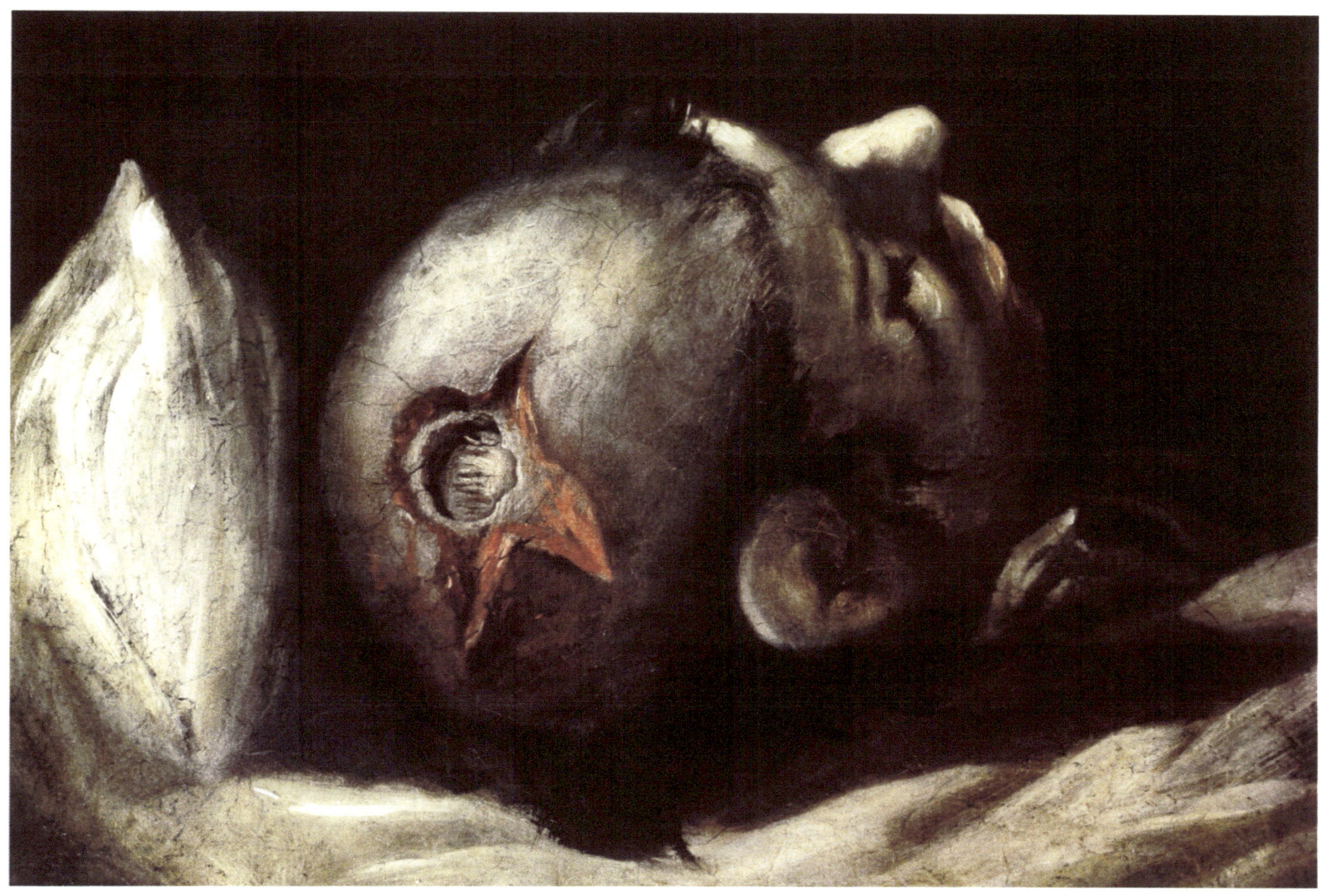

Fig.14 Bullet wound of the skull (33cm x 28cm)

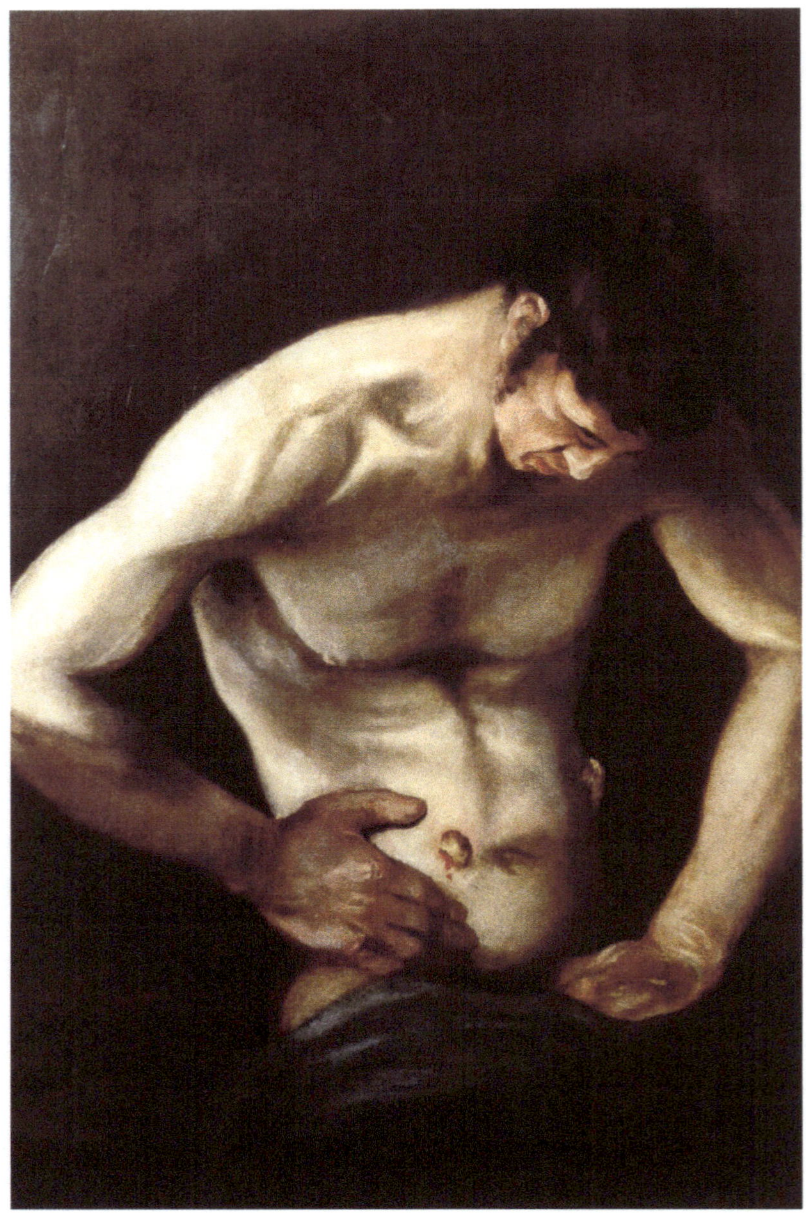

Fig.15 Sketch of a wound of the abdomen (49cm x 58.5cm)

15. Sketch of a wound of the abdomen (49cm x 58.5cm)

Sketch in oil of a wound of the abdomen. This man was safe the ball had not penetrated, it passed under the integuments and the slough which hangs out from the wound is very considerable. This is always the case when the ball runs among the cellular membrane. Another thing we may observe there the larger quantity of slough hangs out from the wound where the ball entered which was here on the left side. The larger quantity of slough which hangs out of the wound and the greater size of the wound at the period of sloughing always indicates that the ball entered there.

Commentary

Bell probably found this case useful for teaching. It was an example of one of the few safer and 'survivable' wounds of the abdomen. There was still a risk of sepsis as the ball would carry in bacteria from the tunic and these would be spread along the missile tract. One feared complication was hospital gangrene, which occasionally spread like wildfire through the 'integuments' (soft subcutaneous connective tissue and fat).

The point Bell makes about the protruding slough is somewhat surprising, yet authoritative. It would be easy to imagine that the ball dragged the tissue through the wound from one side to the other. Thus, the slough would be expected to protrude more through the exit (right-hand) wound. The common thought process at these times was that the exit wound was larger and more ragged than the entry portal.

However, in this case we are probably considering a spent ball. Most of the residual energy of the missile was spent on impact. The tissue damage was therefore maximal at this point, so the slough was more protuberant. The through and through subcutaneous passages of spent balls was a frequent phenomenon. Treatment might consist of excision of the protruding slough and compression dressings by roller bandage.

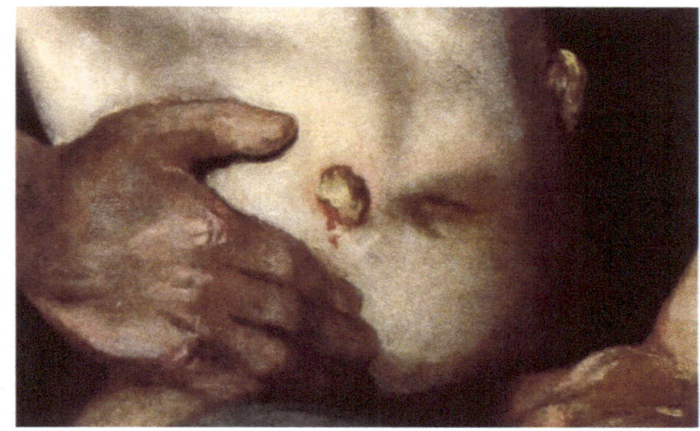

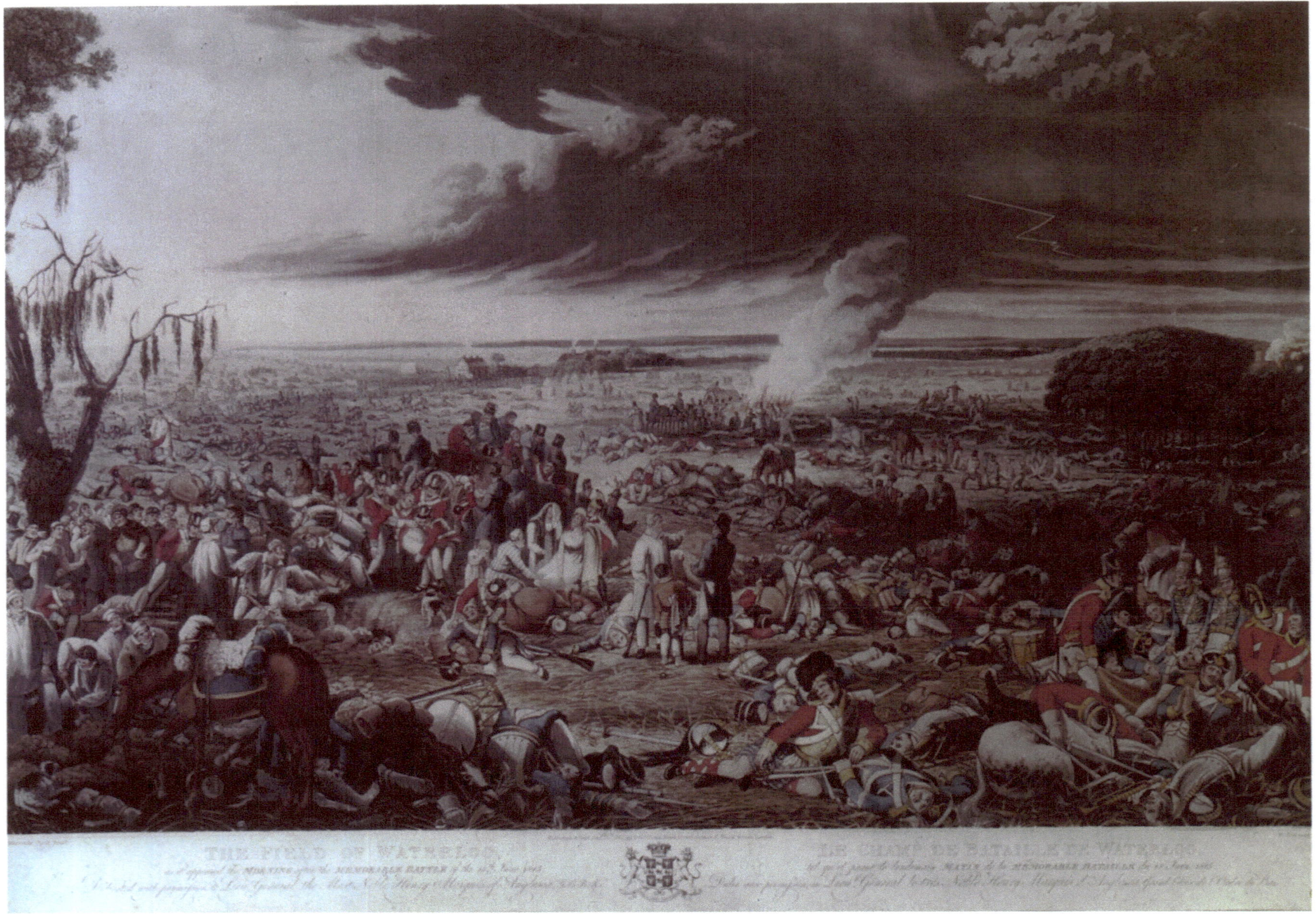

Fig.16 The field of Waterloo in the aftermath of the battle. Courtesy of the Director, National Army Museum, London.

The Battle of Waterloo

The Battle of Waterloo, fought on the 18 June 1815, marked the end of Napoleon Bonaparte and the First French Empire. Bonaparte's last desperate gamble with a cohesive force of 125,000 men (the Armée du Nord) threw assault after assault on the steady but battered Allied forces on the ridge at Waterloo. The steadfast troops, superbly led by Wellington and Blücher, coupled with the rather lacklustre performance by Bonaparte and his generals, won the day. The victory set Britain up as one of the foremost military powers in Europe, in the midst of the immense Industrial Revolution. The lightning campaign of June 1815 encompassed four battles, Ligny, Wavre, Quatre Bras and Waterloo. More than 62,000 men were wounded between the 16 and 18 June. At Corunna the medical support was in its infancy, and after the Peninsular War many of the worn-out, dedicated and now well-honed surgical teams were dissipated and retired to private practice on half pay. There is little doubt that the surgical services in the army and navy had been at their peak at the end of the war in Spain and France in 1814.There were, however, a reasonable number of staff surgeons with field experience at the battle. They were predictably overwhelmed. On the field of Waterloo alone about 55,000 dead and wounded men spread over about three square miles required a good deal more assistance than could be mustered. There was little efficient conveyance and few enough surgeons to meet demand.

Just as after the battle at Corunna, the word went out that there were a large number of casualties. Some surgeons and civilians travelled to Brussels. Bell, Thomson, Somerville, John Shaw and Guthrie were perhaps the most notorious of the group. Bell and his friends reached Dover on 28 June, ten days after the battle. They stayed in Brussels from 30 June to 7 July. Bell and Thomson, although not of the same technical calibre as Guthrie and Hennen, gave invaluable counsel and support after the battle. Baron Dominique-Jean Larrey, arguably the greatest military surgeon of the late eighteenth and nineteenth centuries, assisted in Brussels after some perilous battlefield threats at the hands of the Prussians.

The Waterloo Watercolours

Bell sketched his cases. Originally there were forty-five illustrations (folio volume 15 x 10 inches) in black lead and added in detail with shading and red chalk to emphasise various pathological issues. He eventually condensed these into seventeen watercolour paintings. These sketches are remarkably true to life, and reflect the severe injuries of early nineteenth century warfare.

The first set of watercolour paintings were used for teaching purposes at University College, London. His original sketchbook and the interleaved, annotated edition of his *Dissertation on Gunshot Wounds* are, at the present, missing.

The second set of illustrations were repainted in 1836 when Bell was appointed to the Regius Chair of Surgery in Edinburgh. These paintings measured two and a half feet long and one foot ten inches wide. When Bell left Edinburgh, he took the paintings with him and they were later presented to the Army Medical Department by Lady Bell and displayed on the walls of the pathological museum of the department at Netley Hospital. They now reside on permanent loan in the Wellcome Trust for the History of Medicine.

After each case illustration, Bell added his personal comments and those of some other contemporaries (Alexander Shaw, Bell's brother-in-law). Later comments (Deputy Inspector T. Longmore) are also annotated. Brief modern surgical and military observations on each of the seventeen watercolours are then included.

Where possible, casualty rates are stated throughout, providing a context for these individual cases. There are also some general comments on hospitals, surgeons and, in particular, the wounds these men suffered.

French casualty rates (culled from Digby Smith's book

Napoleon's Regiments: Battle Histories of the Regiments of the French Army, 1792–1815, published by Greenhill Books, 2000) are probably conservative. Referring solely to officer injuries, they only give some indication of general attrition rates.

Preceding the Waterloo paintings was a preface, which follows below. This was written by Sir Thomas Longmore CB in the 1860s and referred to in the Army Medical Department Report (1865) vol. VII. p. 596.

Description of the Waterloo Drawings, Charles Bell's Sketchbook and his Interleaved *Dissertation on Gunshot Wounds* by Sir THomas Longmore CB

DESCRIPTION of a Series of Watercolour Drawings, executed by the late Sir CHARLES BELL, illustrative of Wounds received at the Battle of Waterloo, presented by his Widow to the Army Medical School, together with a sketchbook, Book of Manuscript Notes, and some Original Letters.

By Deputy Inspector General T. LONGMORE, CB, Professor of Military Surgery. [Having served in the line for sixteen years, including the Crimea, Thomas Longmore subsequently held the Chair in Military Surgery, Army Medical School, 1860–61. He became Surgeon General to the Army Medical Department in 1872. He was a prolific writer and died in 1895 – Authors].

In the summer of 1866, Lady Bell, the widow of the late Sir Charles Bell, FRS, presented to the Right Hon. The Secretary of State for War, for the Army Medical School, a series of seventeen large watercolour drawings, executed by her late husband. These drawings are all illustrative of wounds which had been received at the battle of Waterloo. The value of the present was greatly enhanced by the additional gift of the following two very interesting books, both of which had relation to, and served still further to explain, the drawings before mentioned, viz:-

The sketch-book which Sir Charles made use of in 1815, at Brussels, containing the original sketches from which the large watercolour drawings were subsequently executed [missing].

An interleaved copy of Sir Charles Bell's Dissertations on Gunshot Wounds, which he carried with him to Brussels and used as a note-book. This book contains memoranda concerning most of the cases figured in the watercolour drawings [missing].

Six interesting original letters, written from Brussels to Mr Charles Bell during the months of August and September 1815, and having reference to the progress of some of the cases depicted in the sketch-book, were also included in the present by Lady Bell.

One of these letters is signed by J. Hennen, two by C. Collier, one by J. Boggie, one by H. Blackadder, and one by J. Roche – names of eminent military surgeons familiar to all who have studied the history of military surgery during the period of the Peninsular wars [missing].

Lastly, the collection was rendered more complete from being accompanied by a descriptive catalogue of the cases forming the subjects of the drawings, as far as information concerning them could be obtained, arranged by Mr Alexander Shaw, Surgeon of the Middlesex Hospital, and brother-in-law of Sir Charles Bell. The materials of this catalogue, as mentioned by Mr Shaw, were obtained by him from several sources, viz:-

Notes in pencil by Sir Charles Bell himself, written on the margins of the original drawings in his sketch-book.

Letters from the surgeons who were subsequently in charge of the patients. Notes written on the interleaved copy of the Dissertations on Gunshot Wounds (These three sources have been before referred to as part of Lady Bell's present to the Army Medical School.)

Sir Charles Bell's work entitled Surgical Observations, the first quarterly part of which was published in 1816.

A manuscript catalogue of the museum of the Royal College of Surgeons of Edinburgh, in which some of the cases which are the subjects of the drawings are referred to.

The histories of the cases, so far as they are noticed in the following account of the drawings, are abridged from Mr Shaw's catalogue.

The value of these acquisitions to the Army Medical School, whether regarded simply as works of art, or in their relations to the history of military surgical science and practice, or as souvenirs of the handiwork of the distinguished author of the Anatomy of Expression, can hardly be over-estimated.

It may perhaps be of service to make the nature and particular character of this gift to the Army Medical School generally known and with this view I forward a somewhat detailed description of the several books and drawings above enumerated.

Sir Charles Bell's Sketchbook

This is a folio book, 15 inches long by 10 inches in width; 46 pages are covered with pencilled sketches illustrative of 45 cases of wounds observed by Sir Charles Bell in the hospitals at Brussels, shortly after the Battle of Waterloo.

On the first page of the book is a drawing of Shakespeare's Cliff, Dover, with a note observing that he reached Dover early on 28th of June, 1815. Mr Shaw mentions that Sir Charles Bell's visit to the hospitals at Brussels extended from the morning of the 30th June to that of the 7th July, so that the majority of the patients from whom the drawings were made did not come under Sir Charles's observation till between the twelfth and nineteenth days after their wounds had been received.

The drawings in this book are generally outline sketches, slightly shaded, in black lead. The particular parts wounded, the situations where amputation has been performed, the parts swollen or inflamed, are coloured by the addition of red chalk. The 17 watercolour drawings have been selected from these 45 cases in the sketch-book. On the same pages of the sketch-book on which the drawings appear, are usually a few notes of the histories of the cases represented, the names of the hospital in which the patients were placed, and a few other such particulars. Occasionally there are memoranda concerning some special features in the symptoms or nature of the case which had attracted Sir Charles Bell's attention. Now and then the sketch of the patient, and of the superficial appearances of his wound, are accompanied by a diagram showing the supposed injury inflicted in the deeper anatomical structures at the seat of the injury. The memoranda noted are often very brief; as, for example, such a remark as the following:- 'Remember the short cough and the sound of air spurting at the same time from the wound.' Sometimes the drawings have evidently been made not so much to note the appearances of wounds of special interest, as to show some examples of injudicious surgery. An interesting instance of this appears on page 7 of the sketch-book. On this page is a drawing of a patient with an amputated thigh. The stump has a circular bandage round it; but no skin or flaps whatever have been left as a covering for the surface of the stump, the whole aspect of which is fully exposed to view. The patient is lying in bed with his back and head elevated, and the stump slightly bent upwards; he is pressing upon a compress over the site of the femoral artery near the groin, with the thumb of his left hand, while he supports the stump below with his right hand. Near the exposed face of the stump is a pad of charpie, marked A, which appears as if recently taken off from it. The following memoranda are inscribed on the page with this drawing:- '30th. A l'Hôpital de Gendarmerie. Bleeding; took off the dressing; bleeding stopped. This is a Frenchman; amputated on the field. The stump bleeding, it was necessary to open the wound; but it was open, and, under the rags, only this (A) clotted mass of charpie on the face of the stump. The wretched man understands a great deal: he keeps his thumb fixed on the compress over the artery: he says that the artery was tied, but "qu'il est tombé." This is a venous haemorrhage, from the veins being compressed. Here is an hospital mate, who says, "well, they cut them like a round of beef." The limb is directly off, and the whole on the same level; the bone projecting; the skin not retracted. By-the-bye, the surface remarkably healthy, and in good state of granulation. Found this quite historical, for it is far behind…'

On the next page is the drawing of a patient who has had the radius and ulna of his left arm fractured by a bullet, which has afterwards coursed under the skin of the abdomen, and lodged in the hypogastric region. The left hand is shown to be greatly enlarged, and the notes state, 'The hand swollen by the bandage around the broken arm.'

Sometimes touches of character are noticed. Thus, in connection with a severe wound of the abdomen, with visceral protrusion, there is the remark, 'A Frenchman, in great spirits, and of course in fine contrast with that pale Dutchman.'

The sketches, however, of chief interest are those selected for representation in the more highly-finished watercolour drawings. Although the illustrations in the sketch-book are comparatively lightly finished, and bear the marks of the rapid, sketchy manner in which they were executed, they will repay a very careful examination. In each instance a consciousness of the faithfulness of the whole picture at once arrests the attention of an observer. The perfect knowledge of anatomy shown in the outlines – the natural positions in which the patients are lying, or the injured limbs reposing – the expression of the features, in many instances specially characteristic of the particular injury, or of the particular state of the patient in the case represented – show at once the accomplished surgeon and the master-hand of a thorough artist.

In addition to the surgical illustrations just mentioned, the sketch-book contains many plans and drawings of the ground on which the battle of Waterloo had been fought, and the appearance presented by it at the time of Sir Charles Bell's visit to Brussels. These drawings are taken from different points of view, and accompanied with numerous annotations written in pencil.

Sir Charles Bell's *Dissertation on Gunshot Wounds*

The printed matter of this volume is identical with section xvii, On Gunshot Wounds, of the second edition of Sir Charles Bell's System of Operative Surgery, founded on the Basis of Anatomy, published in London in 1814, the year before the battle of Waterloo took place. Some copies of this section were struck off and published separately from the large work, the title and numbering of the pages being alone changed, and this is one of them.

The particular copy presented to the Army Medical School is plentifully interleaved, and many notes, written both in pencil and in ink, are scattered through it; but a large proportion of the inserted pages are still blank. Although not so stated in writing, the internal evidence is quite sufficient to show that most of the notes contained in the book were written at the time the observations were made to which the notes refer, or very shortly afterwards. The notes are frequently dated, and often written in the present tense, thus: '2nd July, Brussels. Let any man go into the hospital of —, and observe the manner in which the wounded are lying; he will be aware of the distracting difficulties the surgeon has to contend with, if there be no arrangement.' 'Tuesday, July 3, there were very many important cases; see sketches.' 'The wounded officers are very ill arranged. They ought to be together; if not in a house, in a street or quarter. But let me not be mistaken; it is of the first consequence that the patients should be dispersed, &c …'

At the end of the book is a short and hurriedly written diary, in which notes are made of some of the most important operations performed by Sir Charles Bell himself in the hospitals. These are illustrated by a few pen-and-ink sketches. One of the last entries in this diary is of particular interest, as regards the history of the case to which it refers; for the description given, though brief, agrees in all particulars with the history of the celebrated case of the French soldier whose thigh Mr Guthrie successfully amputated at the hip-joint at Brussels, at 2 p.m. on the 7th July, the day on which Sir Charles Bell left Brussels. The broken and separated head and neck of the femur belonging to the case in question is specimen No. 2,929 in the Pathological Museum of the Army Medical Department at Netley. The entry in Sir C. Bell's note-book is the following: 'The last case I observed in this "hôpital" was a wound in the groin, which shattered the head of the thigh bone. Here the shot entered [a slight drawing follows, with a line pointing to the opening, which appears in the sketch to be just over the greater trochanter], and the head of the bone I discover to be fractured and separated from the shaft.'

'My proposal is to extract the head of the bone, and do no more. Mr Guthrie's proposal is to amputate the thigh at the hip-joint. If the bone be taken out, there is a great cavity and suppuration certainly; but by this means the shock and violence will be saved. I fear the shock of so great an injury, especially as now the wound cannot be cut off, and its injury must be super-added to that of the incision. The man will readily allow of my proposal, but not of G's. However, next day he said that he would consent. In the meantime I was forced home by business. I had some officers to see, &c …'

*This note thus appears to show that Sir Charles Bell anticipated the present views with regard to the least unpromising plan of treatment for such an injury. The wound in the case in question was just that for the treatment of which resection of the head and neck of the femur would now be recommended by most surgeons, instead of the almost certainly fatal proceeding by amputation at the hip. Indeed, resection was actually and successfully performed in an almost exactly corresponding case in the Crimea, by Surgeon O'Leary of Her Majesty's 68th Regiment; and has since been done with success in four instances, during the late war in the United States, for wounds of a similar nature.**

The Watercolour Drawings

These drawings, seventeen in number, and life size, are painted on paper about two feet and a half long, by one foot ten inches in width, with slight variations. They were done by Sir C. Bell when he was appointed Professor of Surgery in the University of Edinburgh, in 1836, and were used as illustrations for his lectures. As before mentioned, they were selected and enlarged from the drawings of wounds in the sketch-book previously described.† They are all executed with remarkable freedom and vigour, and both their style and colouring cause them to be most effective at the distance at which the drawings are usually exhibited.

Most of the wounds represented are wounds by gunshot; some few are sabre wounds. They have been selected so as to illustrate wounds of each of the principal regions of the body, viz: head, four; face, one cartoon, with two illustrations; neck, two; chest, one; abdomen, one; upper and lower extremities, eight; total, seventeen. The wounds are not exhibited in their most recent state, but in the condition in which they appeared between the twelfth and nineteenth days after they had been inflicted – after various consequences, local and general, had been induced.

A short notice of each of the cases illustrated follows. They are described seriatim, according to the regional distribution of the wounds, as well as in accordance with the numbers borne on the drawings themselves.

** See Tabular Statement of Excisions of the Head of the Femur for Gunshot Injury, &c…Circular No. 6, War Department, Surgeon-General's office, Washington, November 1865, page 62.*

† Mr Shaw mentions that 'another set of copies from the original sketches nearly the same in regard to the selection of the figures, but in comparison less carefully executed, were made some years before by Sir Charles Bell, on his appointment to be Lecturer on Surgery, in University College, London. This collection is still in the Museum of University College.' [These are not to be found in the museum – authors.]

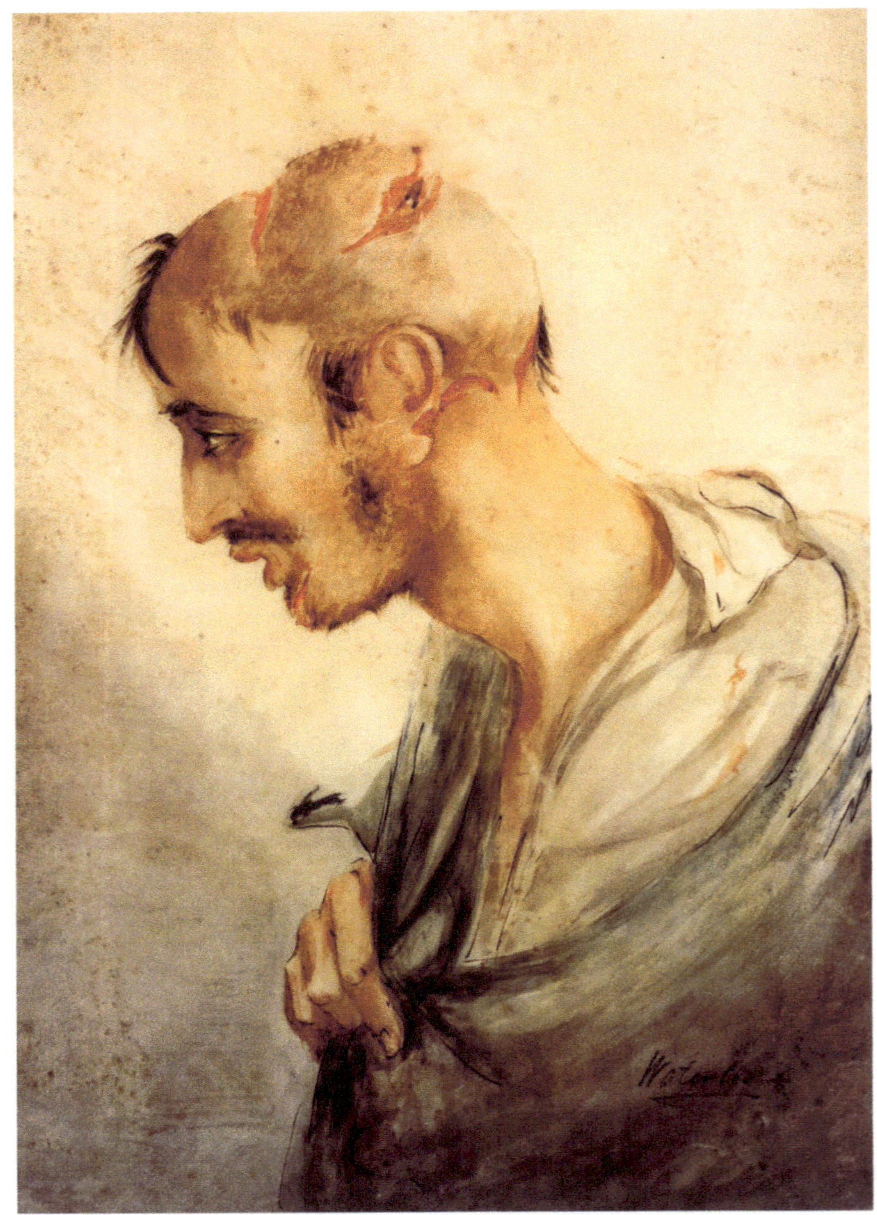

Fig.17 (Head) Trooper 1st or Royal Dragoons

1. (Head) Trooper 1st or Royal Dragoons

Notes and Case History

Sabre wound. A portion of the skull at the vertex completely detached by the sabre-cut; the corresponding part of the scalp remains connected by a small isthmus.

The original sketch is in page 2 of the sketchbook. On the same page is a drawing of the 'piece of bone taken away,' and a sketch of a skull, showing the position of the removed portion. There are also the following pencil marks on this page: – 'Hop. De la Gendarmerie, 5th July. This man was brought into the hospital insensible. None of the soldiers knew him; he can only tell that he belongs to the 1st Dragoons. This portion of the bone was completely detached, and a quantity of matter between it and the dura mater.'

Another note on the same page says, 'On being urged to speak, he makes painful effort to speak but cannot. He can sit up in a chair without support, but stoops languidly and with a vacant and indifferent expression of countenance.' There is an allusion to this case in the notebook: 'The next case was that of a sabre wound in the head, as seen in the sketch. I advised the isolated piece to be taken away, and the integuments to be preserved, which was done. He was considerably relieved in his symptoms the day after the operation, but still could give no account of himself.'

The fragment of bone above alluded to passed from Charles Bell's museum (at Fort Pitt, Chatham) to the College of Surgeons of Edinburgh.

'This is one of the most striking of the series of illustrations. The dull and fatuous expression of the wretched young man's countenance, and the helpless condition to which he has been reduced by the effects of his wound, are most forcibly and painfully depicted in the drawing. Not a quality which one may presume he possessed as the dragoon soldier, physical or mental remains, and the picture is distressing to gaze upon; yet Mr Shaw mentions that he was told by Dr Macleod, who attended this patient after Sir C. Bell's departure from Brussels, that the man ultimately recovered.'

Commentary

It is difficult to determine whether this trooper was on horseback or on foot when he was injured. It is quite probable that his mount was killed. When the soldier fell, he probably lost his helmet, made only of a toughened leather shell. He was then repeatedly sabred from above. The wounds shown are also commensurate with several cuts received on the chin, ear and scalp. It is unlikely that the dura mater was breached, simply because his chances of survival would be minimal with cerebral exposure and reduced resistance to sepsis. His languid behaviour is secondary to temporary injury around the area of the brain bruised by the sabre strike. The wound fell around the area of Broca, that is to say the part of the cerebral hemisphere concerned with speech. As the bruising settled and old blood was absorbed, the cerebral function of this young soldier improved and he probably regained normal mental function. More than a fortnight after the injury, although there is little swelling of the ear and jaw wounds, the soft tissues of the scalp, skin fat and muscle remain swollen and tense. The wound would not have been easy to repair, proper apposition of the wound edges being the main problem. The injury was trimmed to a degree, including detaching the piece of skull, which was saved for posterity! A head bandage would have been applied after a few lengths of adhesive tape were placed on the wound. It is unlikely that the wound was sutured. The policy of primary closure was popular at this time in the Army Medical Department due to considerable concern at the exposure of the skull contents. The bony defect would not have been repaired with any artificial material, as it would be today. There were very sporadic examples of this being done in these wars, with silver plates or coins for example. With more superficial lacerations, there was a low risk of sepsis, as the head and neck has a rich blood supply and the wounds would have been healed in two to four weeks.

The identity of the Mr Shaw mentioned in the case history remains uncertain. It might refer to William Shaw, a member of the hospital staff on duty in Britain who had been called out to Brussels. He served as hospital mate from July 1809. Alternatively, and more probable, Mr Shaw may have referred to Sir Charles' favourite pupil and later friend; John Shaw, who accompanied him to Brussels. It may well be that Dr MacLeod wrote to Shaw later. Dr MacLeod, who attended this trooper after Bell's departure from Brussels, was either Donald MacLeod, a staff surgeon from 1813, or Roderick MacLeod, a hospital assistant to the forces from March 1815. Less likely, it may have been yet another Roderick MacLeod, a hospital assistant in Waterloo from 1814.

The Gendarmerie (Gens d'armerie) hospital was one of the six general hospitals in Brussels caring for Allied casualties. The others were the Elizabeth, Jesuits, Annunciate, Orpheline and Notre Dame hospitals.

The trooper's regiment was part of the much-acclaimed Union Brigade, whose cavalry charge at Waterloo was one of the most notable in British military archives. The Brigade was made up of the Royals, or First Regiment of Dragoons, the (2nd) North British Dragoons (the Scots Greys) and the Inniskilling (6th) Dragoons. This was a truly British representation, consisting of English, Scots and Irish cavalry regiments.

The first significant action taken by this regiment was as part of the great charge against Compte Drouet d'Erlon's 1st Corps, made up of approximately 17,000 men. This action incurred considerable French losses and the repulse of d'Erlon's Corps. The cream of Wellington's heavy cavalry was destroyed as a cohesive unit, however, when it was severely cut up by Jacquinot's Lancers. The regiment was spurred on, not only to do as much damage as possible to d'Erlon's men but also to get to the Great Battery of Bonaparte's guns. This was an insurmountable objective. It is conceivable that this young soldier received his wounds during this massive charge.

The First Dragoons had four officers killed and ten were either wounded or missing. Eighty-six troopers died at Waterloo and eighty-eight were wounded, while nine men went missing. There were 395 sabres on the field, signifying a casualty rate of 50 per cent.

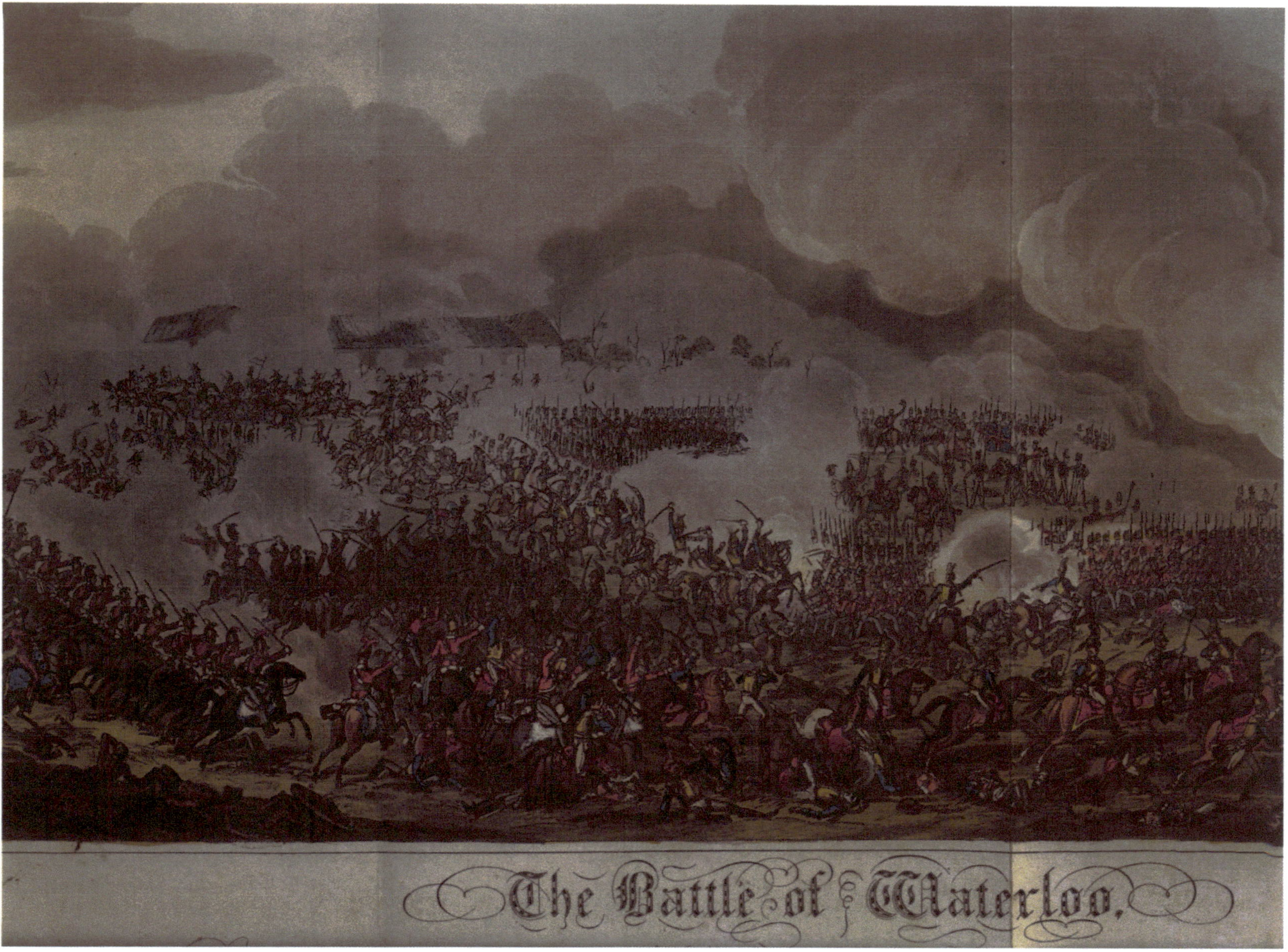

Fig.18 The Battle of Waterloo. 'Delineated under the inspection of officers who were present at that memorable conflict.' W. Mudford, *An Historical Account of the Campaign in the Netherlands*.

2. (Head) Domenic (sic) de Lorraine, 1st Regiment de Ligne

Notes and Case History

'Musket ball wound. The case represented in this forms a remarkable contrast to the preceding one. The patient was shot at the battle of Waterloo. He lay three days on the field without food, was then taken to a village, and from thence to one of the churches in Brussels. He was admitted into the Gendarmerie Hospital, on the 30th of June. The ball entered the cranium in front, passed through part of the brain, lodged behind, and was extracted on the seventeenth day. The patient recovered within two months.' The original drawing is on the third page of the sketch-book, which also has an illustration of a skull, showing the position of the wound of entrance, position of lodgement, and lines of fracture. The notes written in pencil, at different parts of the same page, are the following:

'5th July, Hop. De Gendarmerie. Domenic de Lorraine, 1 Reg. De Ligne. Bones fractured and standing out nearly perpendicularly. The ball, in its exit, struck up the skull; but the bones being resisted by the integuments, the ball rested within the skull. No symptoms of injury to the brain, no dilatation of pupils, no delirium. He is sulky, and complaining of headache; has not been sick; up a good deal, and can walk without support. Complains of being brought down to the operation room, insisting there was no occasion. I withdrew the ball from under the skull with the common dressing forceps. When the ball was shown to him, extracted from under the skull, he expressed satisfaction. Next day he was still well, and was walking about the ward. Under Blackadder's care. Lindsay had a similar case. Durat had also a case of his kind.'

At the end of the interleaved copy of the Dissertation on Gunshot Wounds *used by Sir C. Bell as a note-book, some further memoranda concerning this case occur; and a full report of its subsequent progress, dated August 13th, 1815, in the handwriting of Dr Blackadder, is among the manuscript papers.*

In the drawing, the patient's features are compressed, and indicate a sulky, forced submission to what is going on. There is also an exhibition of some degree of pain. A passage in the note-book thus explains this expression: –'This man had not a symptom. He is quite intelligent. The sketch I made while he was sitting in the chair, he having walked down to the operation room. The expression of pain was not from what he suffered from the wound, nor from the surgeon either; but from the barber of the hospital, who was engaged with him at the time.'

Commentary

This second head injury is interesting in many ways. The patient suffered without decent water and food on the field for three days. By the seventeenth day after receiving his intracerebral injury, he was very lucky to escape serious sepsis. We cannot vouch for the integrity of the meninges (coverings of the brain) but there is no mention of brain tissue being exposed, or of cerebral dysfunction or herniation. He did suffer a headache, unsurprisingly, and could walk unaided. Thus, one is left with the conclusion that the ball was part spent when it struck de Lorraine, missing the frontal sinus and traversing the skull, either passing through the brain substance or travelling between the dura and bone, stripping up the former. It had sufficient force left to strike up the bones perpendicularly, which meant that the missile, having fractured the bones posteriorly (at the back) in the occiput or posterior parietal region, was arrested in its path and lay superficially below the bone, no doubt injuring the dura.

This man would have undergone the rigours of the

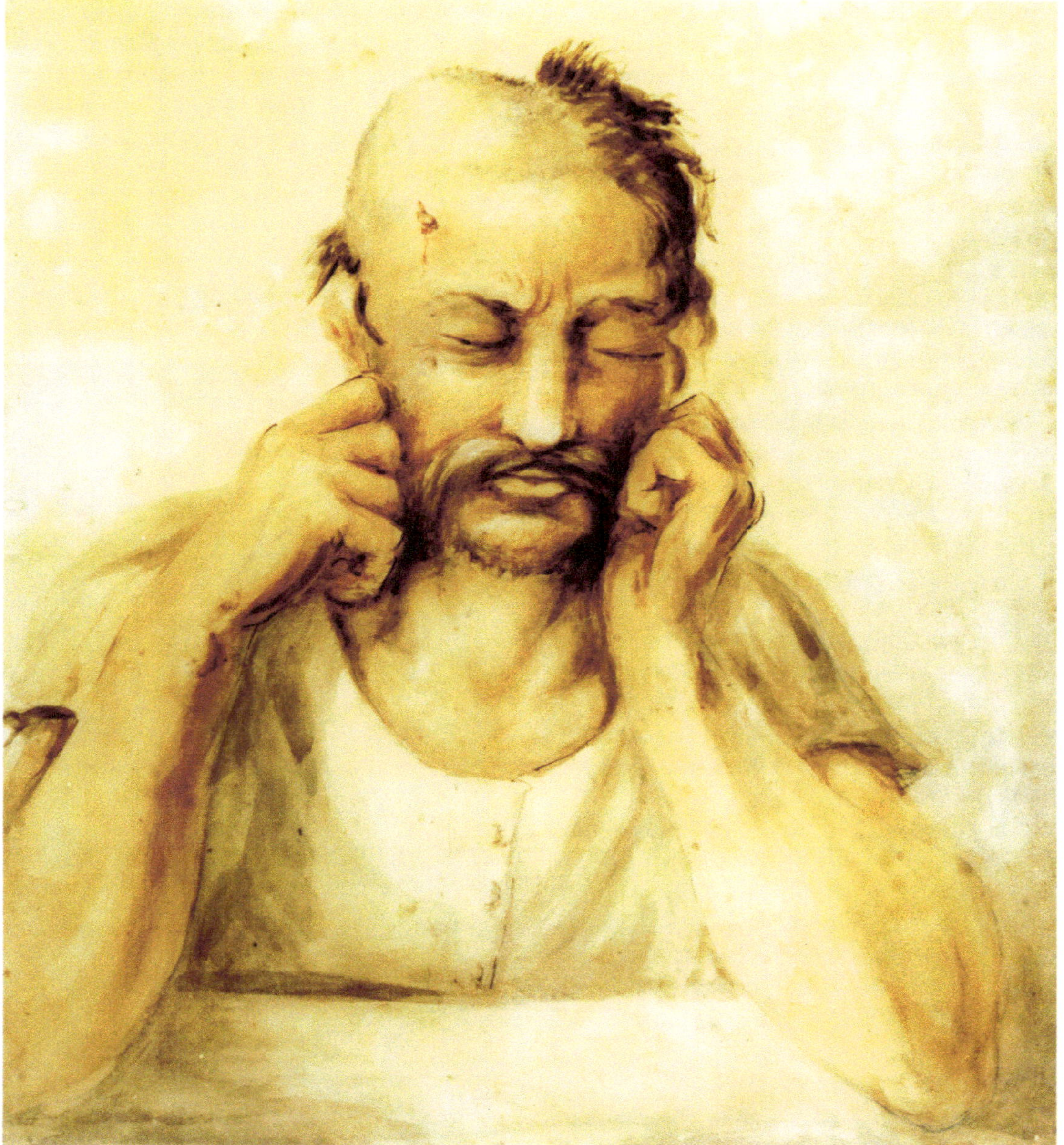

Fig.19 (Head) Domenic (sic) de Lorraine, 1st Regiment de Ligne

antiphlogistic (anti-inflammatory) regimen (bleeding, catharsis and purgation) and then, while sitting on a chair, had his head shaved and the posterior piece of skull removed. The surgeon would take care to preserve as much dura mater as possible. With the ball revealed, using his common dressing forceps, the surgeon then removed it and gave it to the soldier. It appears that the trephine was not employed, as the removal of the 'loose' piece of bone was all that was necessary to tidy the wound and extract the ball. Adhesive tapes or bandages would have been used to close the wound.

The reader is left to decide whether the surgery was as slick and relatively painless as Bell made out, or whether the barber was rather heavy-handed!

The patient was being cared for in the Gendarmerie Hospital. Sir Charles left him under the care of Mr Blackadder, a staff surgeon. Henry Home Blackadder was a hospital assistant with one year's Peninsular experience. After Waterloo, he was promoted to assistant staff surgeon and died young in his thirties, having worked four more years in the army.

Surgeons Lindsay and Durat were also mentioned as having been involved in similar cases. Surgeon Owen Lindsey, although spelled differently from above, fits the bill. He was recalled on full pay on 25 April 1815 as a staff surgeon. He had been a Walcheren and Peninsular veteran. Surgeon Durat has not been identified and was either a seconded French surgeon or, more likely, a Belgian surgeon.

A conclusion as to where de Lorraine was when he was hit on 18 June is difficult. His regiment (the 1st Ligne) was part of the 6th Infantry Division, the largest in the French army at Waterloo. Its size reflected its commander's status, no other than Prince Jerome Bonaparte, also wounded in the battle. This unit had fought in Italy, Wagram, Salamanca, San Sebastian and France.

There were three battalions from this regiment at Waterloo, mustering 1,766 bayonets. The regiment was committed all day to the assault on Hougoumont, on Wellington's right. There was an impressive density of injured around the woods and orchards of the château. Clearance of casualties might well have been slow from this area.

Digby Smith states that there were eleven officers killed and thirty-four wounded in this regiment at Quatre Bras, and Waterloo. De Lorraine may well have been hit during the assaults on Hougoumont.

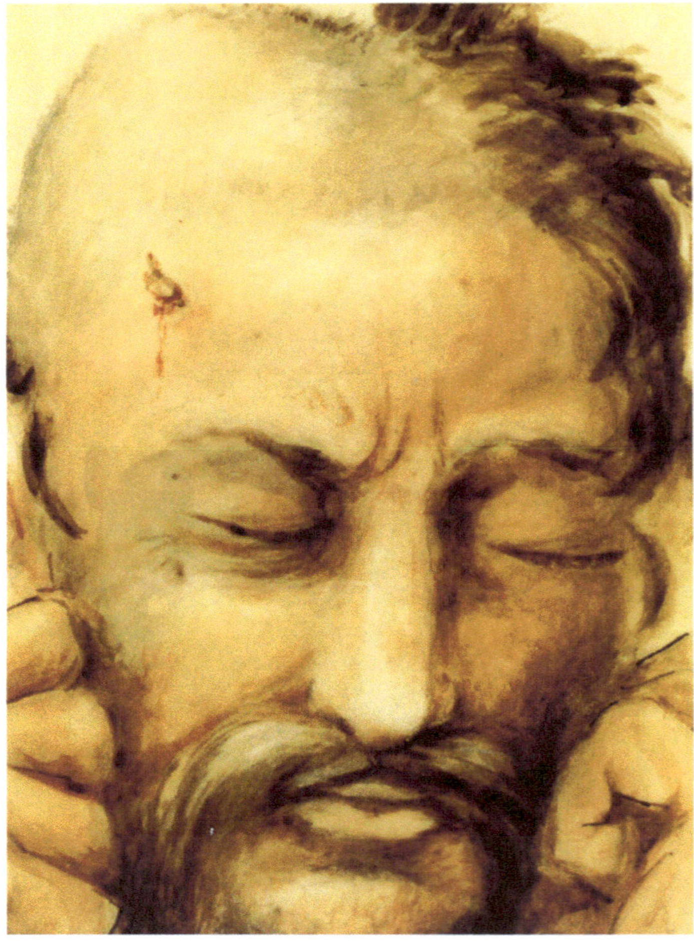

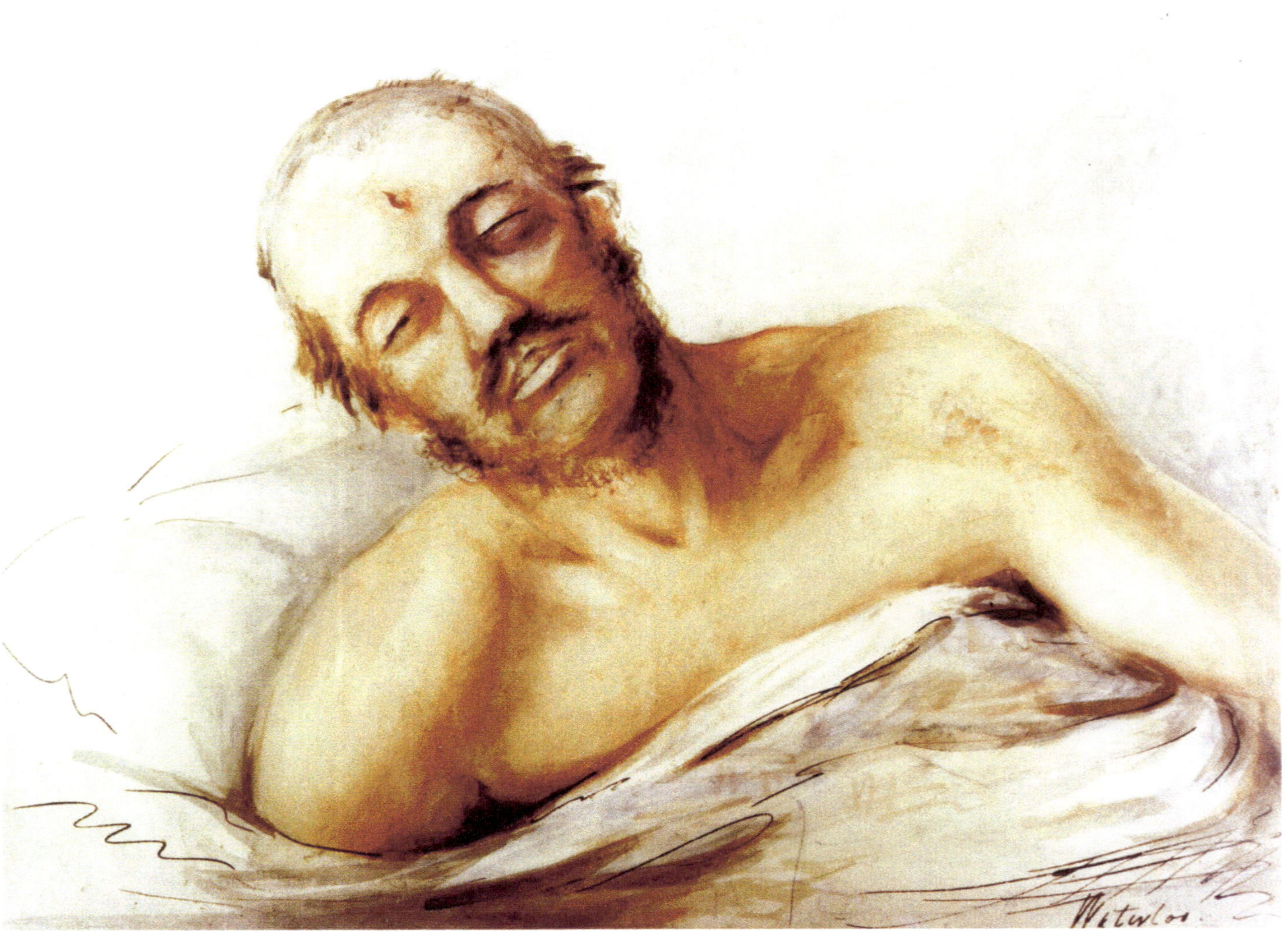

Fig.20 (Head) Samuel Pritchard, 4th Regiment of Foot

3. (Head) Samuel Pritchard, 4th Regiment of Foot

Case Notes and History

Gunshot wound. A musket ball has perforated the frontal bone, entered the left orbit, and is causing protrusion of the eyeball on that side. The following notes appear with the original in the sketch-book:

'June 31. Hop de l'Annunciata. Samuel Pritchard, 4th Regt. assistant surgeon Reid. He has no symptom; you see all. The ball entered here in the forehead. My probe passed three inches and a half, obliquely downwards, and towards the left temple. If I had remained I would have enlarged the wound in the forehead, and taken away the pieces of bone. I would have made an incision into the orbit, and extracted the ball, where I am sure it is lodged.'

Among the collection of letters is one to Mr Charles Bell from Mr J. Roche, dated Brussels, 17th August, in which mention is made that 'Sam Pritchard is alive and doing well … you will perhaps soon have an opportunity of seeing him in England, as he will, I believe, soon be sent home.' The final result of the case does not appear.

The swollen and ecchymosed condition of the integuments covering the protruded eyeball are admirably shown in the drawing. There is no paralysis of the face, but the features wear a peculiarly heavy, torpid aspect.

Commentary

This case is interesting as it illustrates a very high-risk injury. The ball must have passed through the left frontal sinus and lodged behind the left eye, in the orbit. The problem for the patient and surgeon is that there are bacteria carried into the orbit by the ball, both from the skin and the frontal sinus. We have no record of this man's visual loss. There would be a significant threat to the other eye from the condition known as 'sympathetic ophthalmoplegia'. This tragic problem is related to unilateral eye damage, which releases antigens from the damaged iris. Antibodies are raised against these antigens, which then act on the good eye and cause irreversible damage. Thus, in addition to the risk of sepsis, both eyes are lost.

It is hard to imagine how the surgeon could have retrieved this ball without the greatest difficulty. Bell would obviously have made an attempt. The patient, after having the antiphlogistic regimen, would have been operated on in the supine position. There would have been a great need to keep his head steady during this delicate procedure. The surgeon would have enlarged the entrance wound in the forehead and removed any bony fragments and then probably dressed or closed the defect.

He would then have made an incision in the superior (upper) aspect of the orbit and passed a silver probe into the depths of the wound and felt for the click of the probe tip on the lead ball. This would not have been easy, as the probe could have merely hit up against the bony orbit (eye socket). Bullet or dressing forceps would have been inserted into the back of the orbital cavity between the globe of the eye and the bone of the orbit in order to retrieve the missile. During this manoeuvre a finger would depress the globe of the eye to create a little space for the extraction. Wherever the incision into the orbit was made it almost certainly would have resulted in some ocular muscle damage, causing diplopia (double vision) and some defect in movement of the afflicted eye. Pritchard's outcome was favourable. He probably lost the sight from the wounded eye but evidently and remarkably did not succumb from sepsis.

Mr J. Roche was staff surgeon Jordan Roche, who served in the Peninsular from 1814 to 1818. This patient was admitted to the Annunciate Hospital in Brussels.

The 1st Battalion, 4th Foot (King's Own Regiment), was heavily engaged at Waterloo. It formed part of the 10th Infantry Brigade (with 1/40th and 1/27th) commanded by Major General Sir John Lambert in Sir Lowry Cole's 6th Infantry Division. It fielded between 638 and 677 bayonets. The 4th had just returned from America and had only four captains. Initially positioned behind the main Allied field hospital at Mont St Jean, the battalion moved up to Wellington's left during the action. The brigade was not involved at Quatre Bras, but of the 1,325 casualties sustained at Waterloo, 134 were from the 4th Foot.

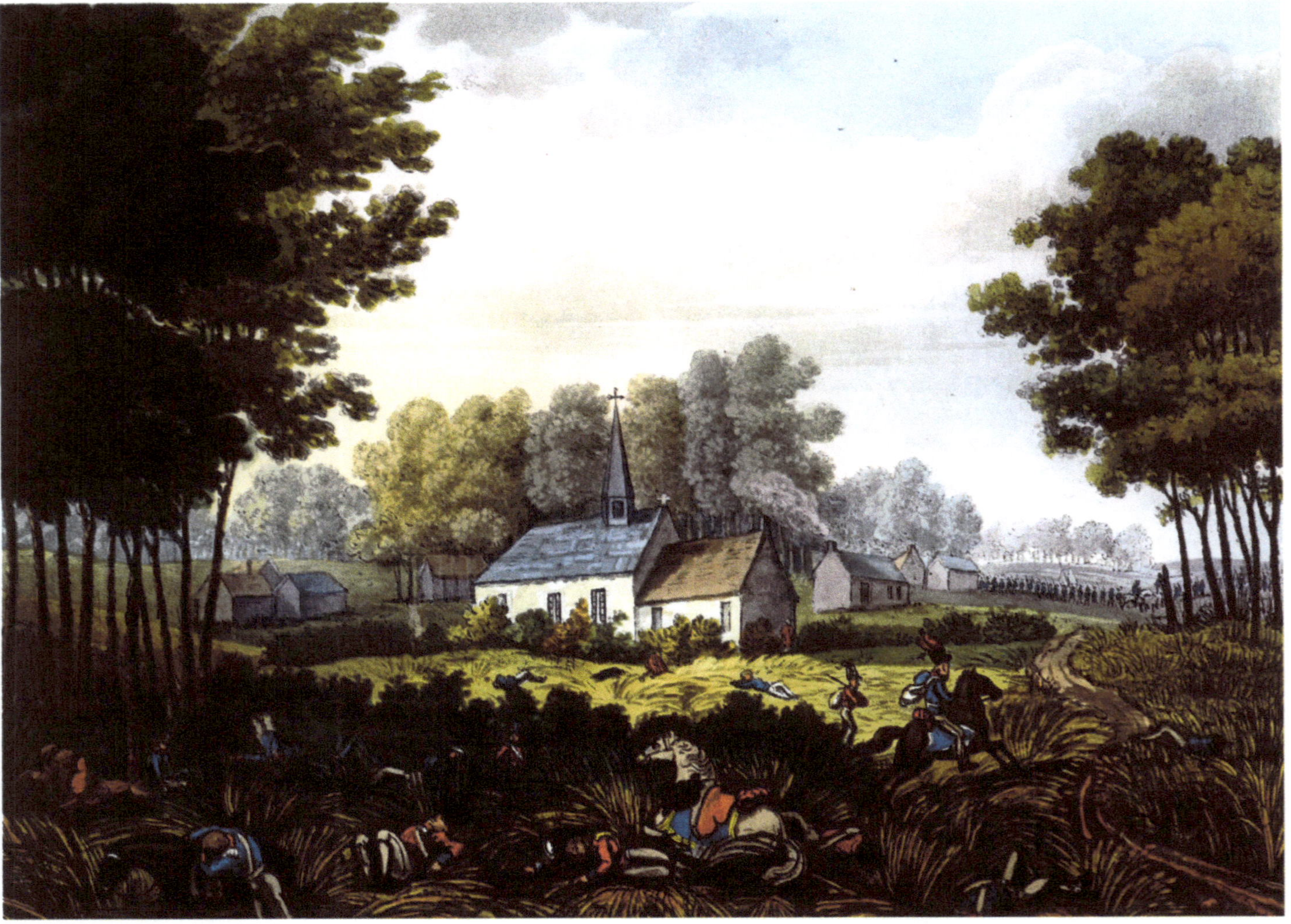

Fig.21 'Chateau of Frischermont. It was on this spot, that Sir T. Picton received his death. Here, also, through the wood, the Prussians under the command of Bulow came up, towards the close of battle.' W. Mudford, *An Historical Account of the Campaign in the Netherlands*.

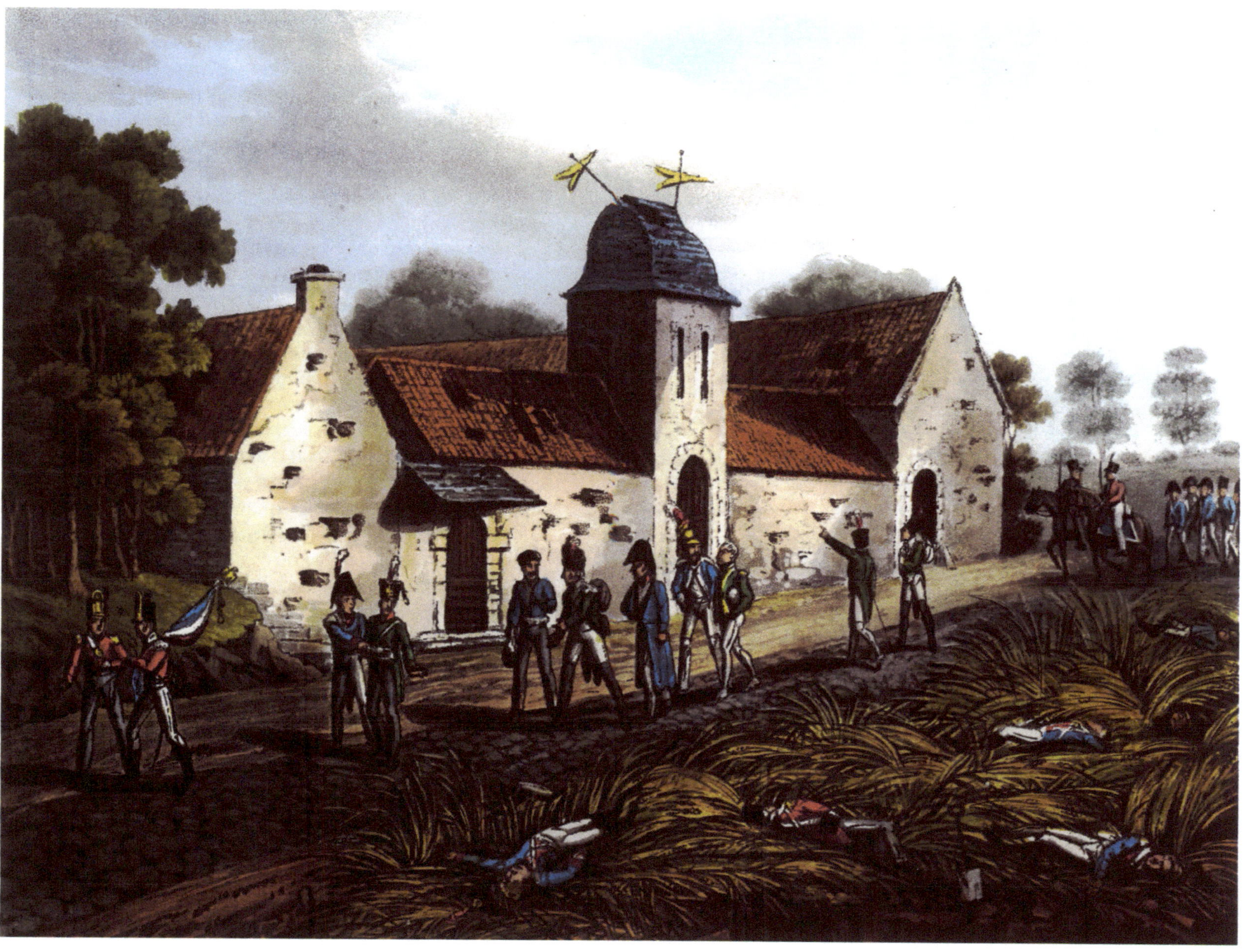

Fig.22 'The farm house of Mont St Jean. This house being close in the rear of the action, it was much dilapidated by random shot.' W. Mudford, *An Historical Account of the Campaign in the Netherlands*.

4. (Head) Wanstell 17th Regiment of Foot

Notes and Case History

Gunshot, fracture of skull. Fungus cerebri. The following are the marginal notes around the original drawing in the sketch-book.

'Caserne Elizabeth, No. 16, sec. D. – Wanstell, 17th Regt. Staff-Surgeon Collyer's [sic – actually Collier] *patient. On the fifth day after the battle was insensible, a portion of the frontal bone, an inch in diameter was found driven into the brain, and it stood perpendicularly; not possible to extract it, from its being firmly wedged. Trepanning performed. Quite insensible during the operation; and showing no sensibility until on the next day, being bled, he shrank.'*

'On the removal of the bone a quantity of blood and brain came out, and coagulum was scooped out from betwixt the skull and dura mater. Three days after the operation he became more sensible, and has been improving. I recommend antimonial solution.' Note pointing to the fungus: – 'pulsating, sloughy.'

The subsequent history of this patient, comprising an account of his death six days after Sir C. Bell had seen him, and the appearances observed at the post-mortem examination, is given in one of the collections of letters, dated Bruxelles, August 5th, 1815, from Mr Collier to Mr Charles Bell. In the drawing the fungus cerebri is very prominent; and the starting eyeballs, open lips, hectic flush of the cheeks, and the general appearance, are strongly indicative of meningeal irritation.

Commentary

As he was still insensible five days after injury, the soldier had obviously suffered a severe head injury. It was a compound wound, with the ball most probably lodged in the brain, but there is no comment on this. It would in most cases have been irretrievable, causing severe bleeding and bruising deep in the cerebral tissue. There is consequent swelling and infection. Since the skull is a rigid box, the swelling can only manifest itself by extruding brain tissue from the skull cavity. This, along with the granulation (healing) tissue and the resultant exudates, is what is termed, 'fungus cerebri.' It should correctly be termed a 'cerebral hernia'.

Surgeons had great difficulty with this injury and its symptoms, as all they could do was to shave off the extruding brain tissue (fortunately a painless process!). There were anecdotal accounts in the Peninsular War of the repeated excision of such tissue, leading in some cases to almost half the cerebral hemisphere being removed. This wound shows evidence of trephining (the cutting out of a circular disc of bone from the skull with a trephine) with a cruciform surgical incision (a cross-shaped cut) in the skin. The only way the surgeon could have removed the wedged piece of bone was by drilling a hole beside the fracture. This would first loosen the fragment, which could then be lifted with a steel skull elevator or spring forceps. Once the barriers of the dura, arachnoid and pia maters (the three coverings of the brain – meninges) were breached, the likelihood of fatal infection in the central nervous system was virtually inevitable. Surgeons were aware of the importance of maintaining the integrity of the meninges, but often they were damaged through injury. In this instance, as was often the case, sepsis was the great killer. Wanstell shows the typical face of a man about to die. This type of expression is called the 'hippocratic facies.' He is grey, haggard and dehydrated and he has an almost wild stare.

This painting is a masterpiece of artistry and, as he often did, Bell captured the tragedy behind the dire clinical problem.

This soldier was hospitalised in the Elizabeth Caserne Hospital in Brussels. He was apparently in bed 16 in D section of the infirmary.

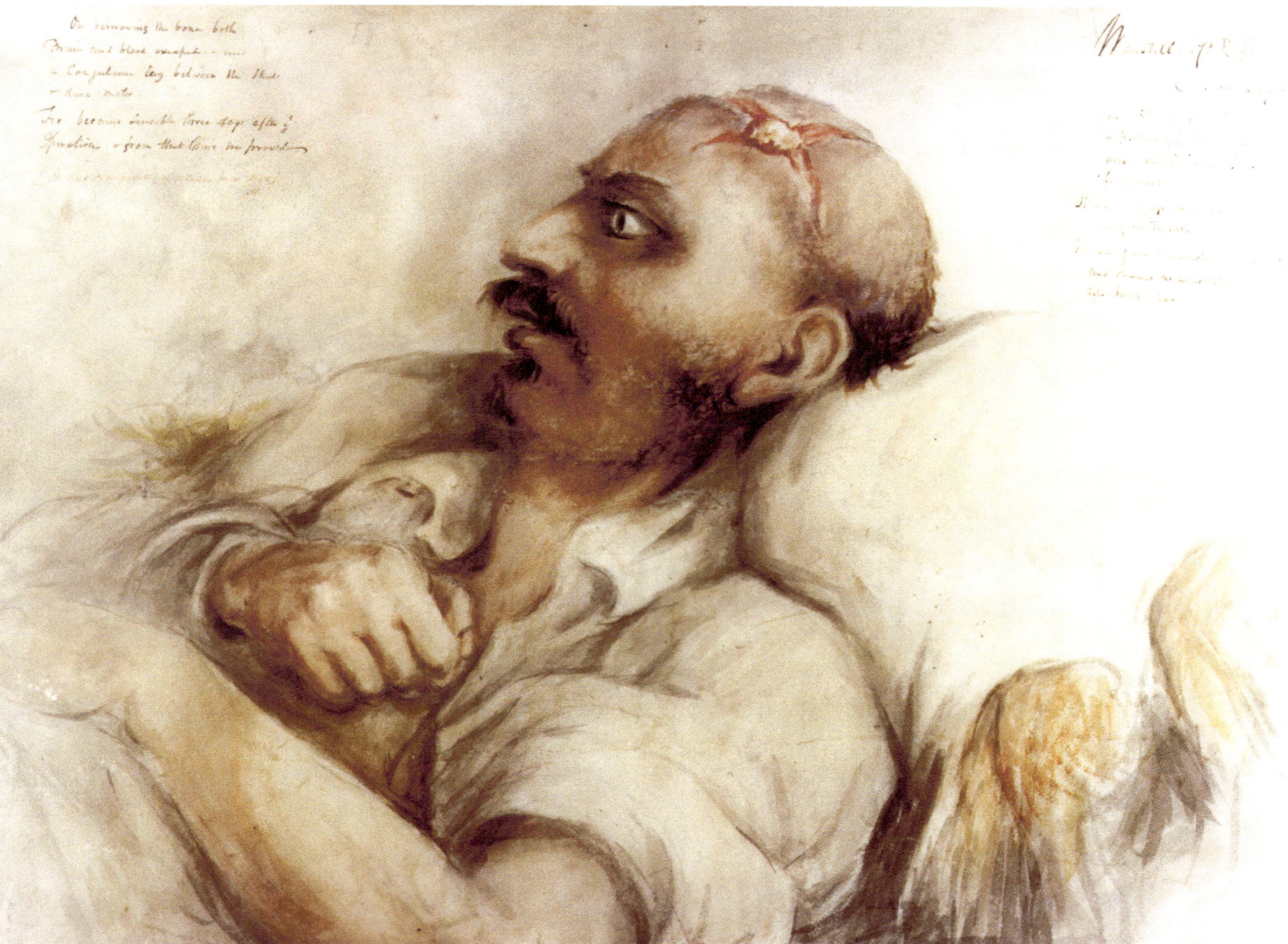

Fig.23 (Head) Wanstell 17th Regiment. of Foot

Wanstell was described as a soldier of the 17th (Leicester) Regiment who were in India and Nepal at this time. It is possible that Bell had the wrong regiment (he might have meant the 1st, 14th or the 27th) or the man was a 'seconded' person, e.g. a bat-man. We have checked the regimental lists of the above three regiments in the Waterloo Medal Roll and cannot find this soldier's name.

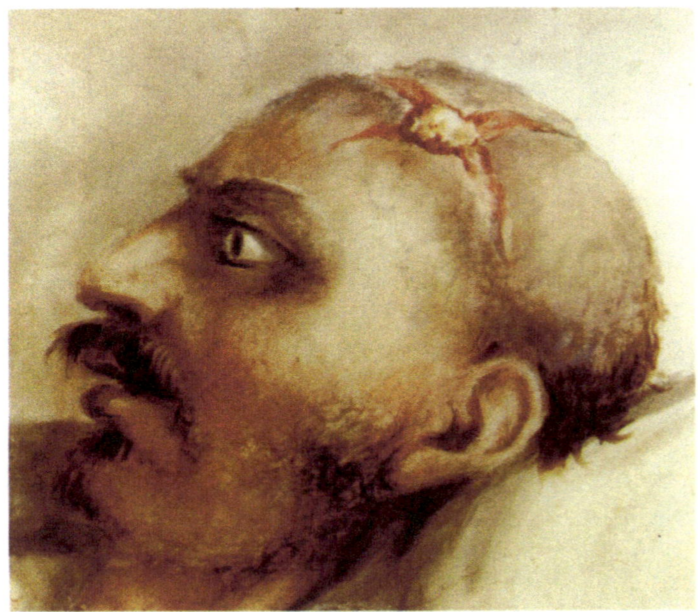

Wanstell 17th Regt

On removing the bone both
Brain and blood escaped - and
a Coagulum lay between the Skull
& dura mater.
He became sensible three days after ye
Operation - & from that time he proved

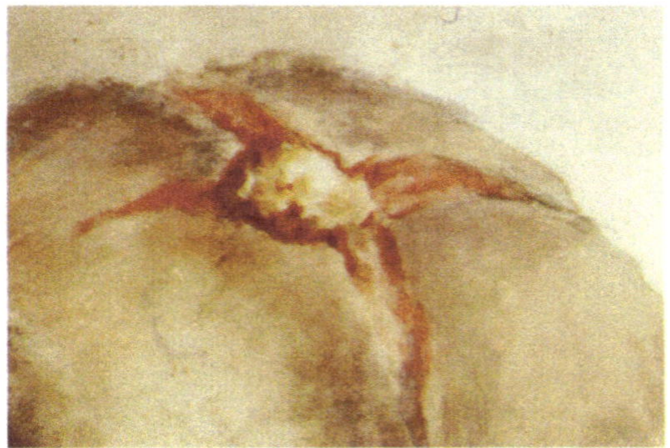

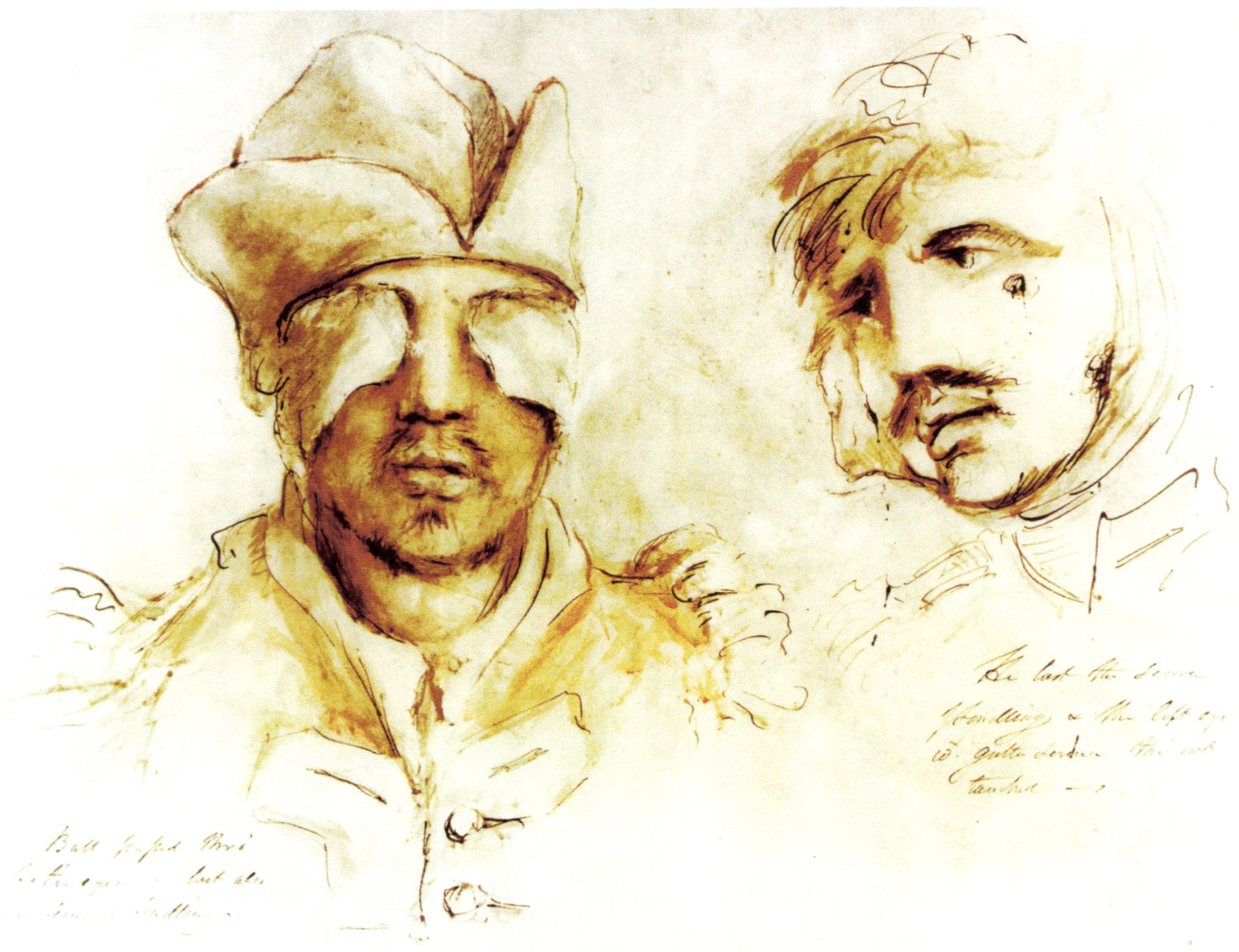

Fig.24 (Face) Two figures

5. (Face) Two figures

Case Notes and History

a) Gunshot wound; penetration of both orbits by a musket ball.

b) Gunshot wound; entrance of projectile over left malar bone.

There are no histories of these cases. The following notes are pencilled down in the sketch-book by the side of the original sketches:

a) 'This through both eyes. This man has also lost the sense of smelling. Deprived of two senses – vision and smell.'

b) 'Another case in the Gendarmerie. This man has lost the sense of smelling. The left eye has gutta serena.'

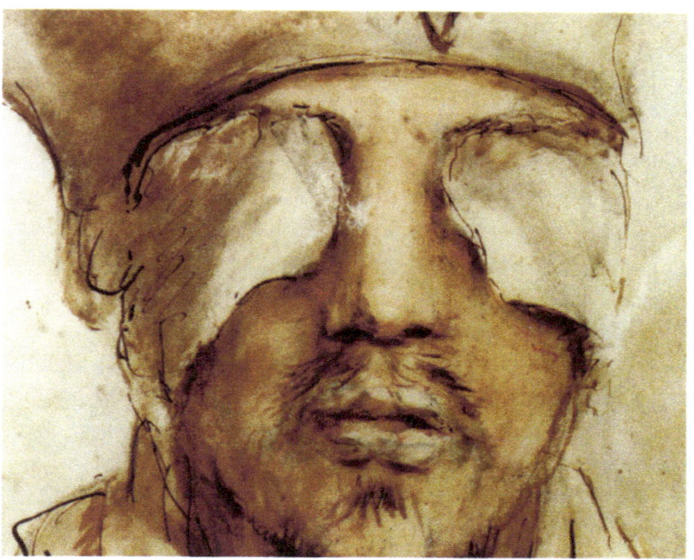

Commentary

These men are among the many who suffered facio-maxillary damage during war. These are British soldiers but their units are not identified. We cannot see the orbital damage to the first soldier. I would assume the ball, fired at moderately close range, passed straight across both eyes, traversing the nasal cavity, fracturing the fragile olfactory apparatus at the roof of the nose, so that the man is blind and anosmic (has no sense of smell).

The second soldier has received a spent ball injury. The ball passed upwards through the maxilla (cheekbone), into the antrum (sinus). It has then broken the olfactory plate (just as in the first soldier).The patient has lost his pupillary reflex and cannot see. The optic nerve has been destroyed. Gutta serena is an older medical term indicating a type of blindness arising from a 'morbid state of the retina or optic nerve.'

The missile in this case is retained and probably lies at the floor of the orbit, posteriorly. This would have caused considerable pain and persistent sepsis. The danger would have been from the infection tracking into the base of the brain.

6. (Neck) Sword wound: penetration of the oesophagus. Trois Louis Celestine, 21st Regiment de Ligne

Notes and Case History

'Hopital de la Gendarmerie, 2nd July. This man and another of the same name were stabbed with the small-swords of English officers.

This wound is betwixt the sterno-cleido tendon, in the centre, and below the cricoid cartilage. The trachea may be wounded, but there is no air passing out. The oesophagus is evidently wounded, for almost the whole food passes this way, and the saliva keeps trickling.'

These are the notes attached to the original sketch in the book.

Commentary

It is uncommon to read of wounds caused by the points of officers' swords. They were relatively ineffectual as chopping weapons and were mostly used for stabbing. They would cause a small diameter entry wound with deep injury. This is a good example of this type of injury. The wound was probably about 3cm to 5cm in depth and may have been arrested by the blade hitting the cervical vertebrae. The sword tip fortunately missed the trachea (windpipe) but pierced the oesophagus (gullet), causing a partially circumferential injury.

The consequence of this was that saliva, liquids and food would exit through the wound site. The initial danger was from infection spreading out from the spillage of contaminated material from the lumen (inside) of the oesophagus into the soft tissues of the neck. Amazingly, this did not happen to any remarkable degree. This is an illustration made from a sketch taken two weeks after the injury. There is little apparent swelling or redness.

The fistula (communication between skin and gullet) resulting from the wound meant that much of the saliva from the mouth and nourishment taken orally would egress from the entry wound. There is absolutely no reason why this fistula and wound should not have healed up completely. So long as there was some continuity of the gullet, the preferential direction for the contents of the oesophagus was via the normal route. Thus, after four to six weeks the patient would make a good recovery from his fistula. Had the wound traversed the trachea, it is unlikely that the patient would have survived.

Celestine has clearly lost weight and wears the typical linen headwear that so many hospitalised patients were supplied with. This was to cover the head, which was usually shaved (although not in Celestine's case) to reduce the chance of verminous infestation.

This soldier was also in the Gendarmerie Hospital in Brussels.

Count Drouet d'Erlon commanded the 1st Army Corps, which contained the Third Division, to which the 21st Regiment belonged. This regiment was commanded by Baron Pierre Louis Binet de Marcognet. The 21st Regiment de Ligne was heavily engaged in the second phase of the Battle of Waterloo. It had two battalions (the 1st and 2nd) and was under the command of Colonel Baron Carre, who was wounded. The regiment fielded 1,137 bayonets and was hit hard during the advance. The corps moved in broad columns and formed into line just as they approached the ridge on Wellington's left. It is likely that Celestine was wounded during this assault, as there were heavy casualties in this brigade. Seven out of eight battalion commanders and one regimental commander were wounded. Digby Smith states the battalion's officer casualties as seven dead and sixteen wounded. The 3rd Division faced Pack's brigade on the ridge at the left of Wellington's line and were badly mauled by the charge of the Union Brigade.

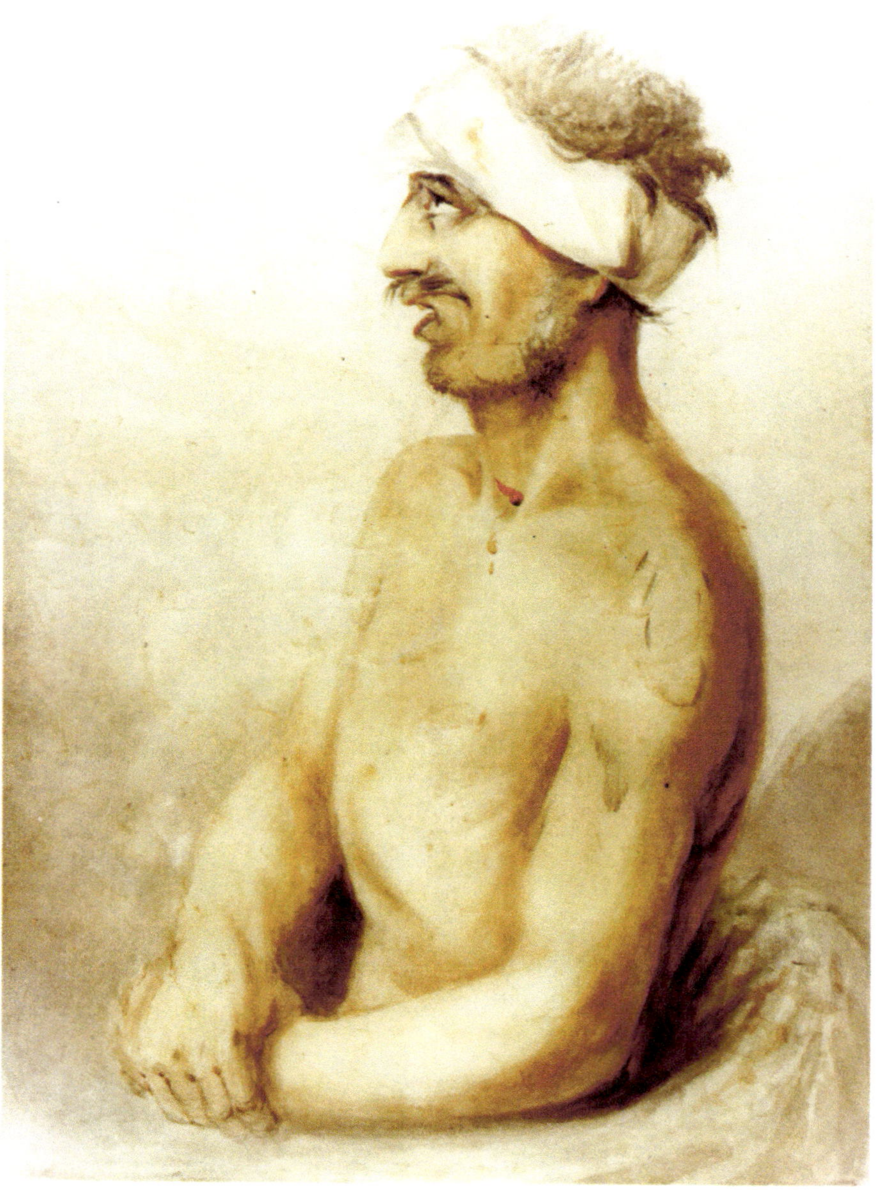

Fig.25 (Neck) Sword wound: penetration of the oesophagus. Trois Louis Celestine, 21st Regiment de Ligne

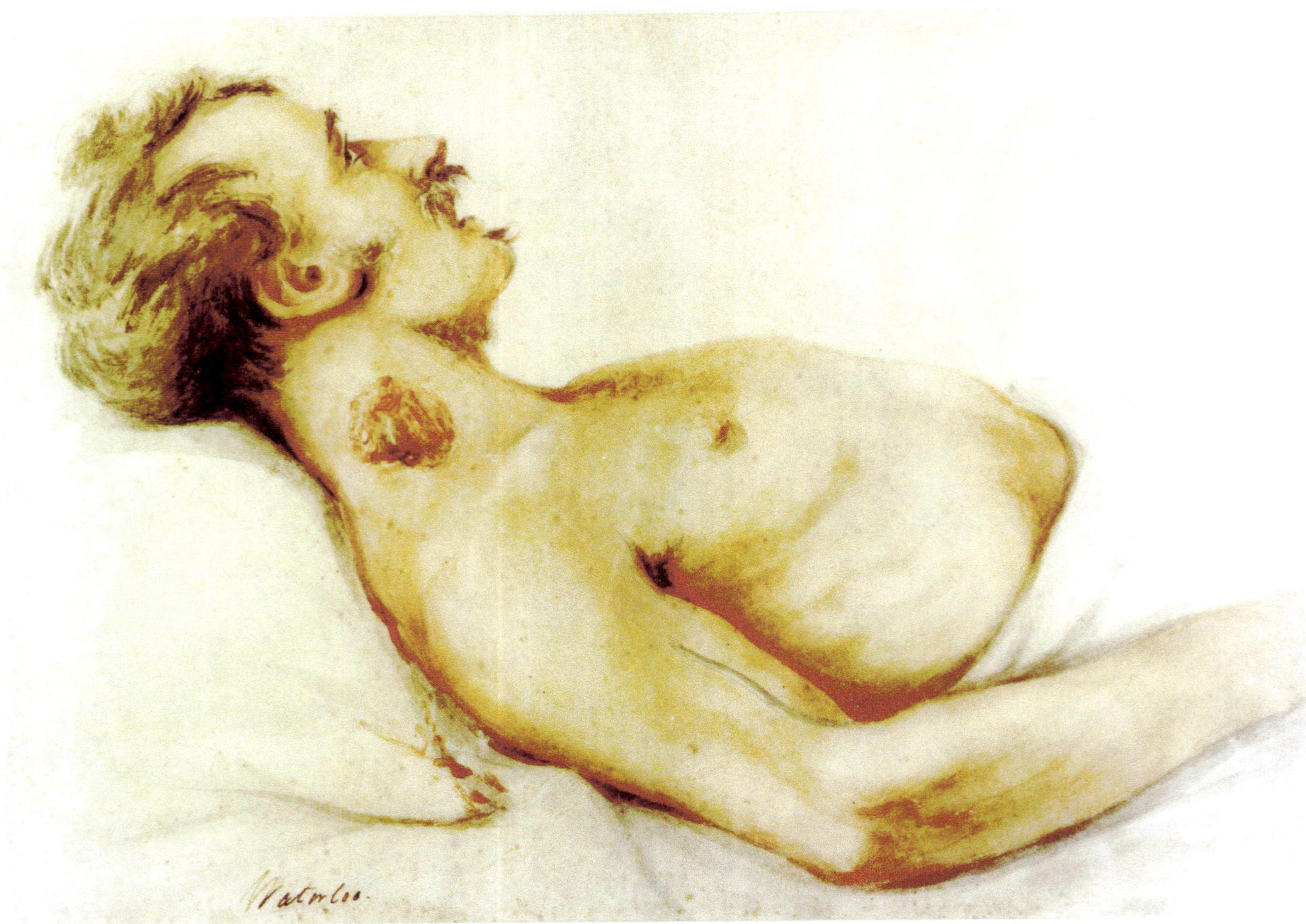

Fig.26 (Neck) James Alexander, 1st Regiment, Royal Dragoons

7. (Neck) James Alexander, 1st Regiment, Royal Dragoons

Notes and Case History

Deep perforating wound of the right lower half of the neck from grapeshot. The following notes are pencilled with the original sketch, from which this drawing was made: – 'Elizabeth Caserne. No. 13 sec. D. James Alexander, 1st Regt. Rl. Dgns. Struck by grapeshot; considerable bleeding on receiving the wound; since several bleedings; the large cavity filled with coagulum, and the bandages soaked; stopped by cold applications; has been bled for pain in the chest, and relieved.'

'There has been no bleeding from the wound for these last three days. The wound will admit the hand! The sterno-cleido, the scalenus, the trapezius seen distinctly; the nerves also, but covered with slimy granulations. The beating of the carotid distinct in the wound, pumping up the matter. The right arm tumid and paralytic. I am asked how he is to proceed in [the] *event of returning haemorrhage.'*

A line marking 'exit of the ball' points to a wound a little above the right acromion.

The conclusion of this case is mentioned in one of the letters to Mr Bell, dated Bruxelles, August the 5th 1815 and signed Charles Collier. 'James Alexander did not survive forty-eight hours after you saw him. I was quite prepared, in the event of haemorrhage, to cut down upon and secure the bleeding vessels; but he died exhausted. He died as I have seen many, from the powers of life yielding to an injury they are unable to repair. He has no fever or cough.'

In connection with this case Sir Charles Bell has related the following anecdote of Baron Larrey: 'On looking over my sketches of the wounded at Waterloo with Baron Larrey, he fixed with interest on the case of a young man who had been wounded in the lower part of the neck. "Well I know", says this excellent surgeon, "how that man must have died. I have seen many wounded so in my campaigns, and die from air drawn into the veins."' (Practical Essays by Sir Charles Bell, Edinburgh, 1841, p. 11).

Commentary

This is a fascinating clinical problem, in the main because the patient survived on the field. The initial haemorrhage was great and it was probably Alexander's profound shock that lowered his arterial blood pressure so much that the bleeding eventually ceased. Perhaps he or a comrade pressed on his wound somehow to aid haemostasis. He obviously had further bleeds from the wound after his retrieval. The wound was covered in clots, which at the time prevented further haemorrhage.

Why did the patient have chest pains? Was this due to angina from the profound haemodilution (anaemia resulting from loss of red blood cells which carry oxygen)? Did his symptoms improve because he bled out so much that he fainted? If the picture is carefully inspected, the brachial (nerve) plexus is visible and the carotid pulsations had been noted in the depth of the wound. The main cluster of nerves leaving the neck to supply the upper limb muscle was not only visible, but clearly severely damaged. Collier was obviously prepared to spring rapidly into action should severe secondary bleeding occur. He would have exposed the common or external carotid artery and pulled it up with a tenaculum or dressing forceps. A ligature would then have been thrown around the vessel.

The right cephalic vein can be clearly seen on Alexander's arm. It is either turgid with venous blood or thrombosed since the right subclavian vein has clearly been damaged by the shot. It is obstructed and there is no flow up the vessel so it is therefore prominent. It is difficult to know if the ball injury damaged the left internal jugular or the left subclavian vein.

Perhaps the most interesting aspect of the poor man's story is illustrated in the comments made by that surgical master of the Napoleonic Wars, Baron Dominique-Jean Larrey. He assisted with the injured after Waterloo and prior to this had been taken prisoner and almost (mistakenly) executed by the Prussians. He had instantly recognised the likely cause of Alexander's death – air drawn into the veins. This may be one of the first descriptions of fatal air embolism. Approximately 200cc of air need to be immediately injected into the circulation to bring about cardiac dysfunction and arrest. If Alexander had become dyspnoeic (had difficulty in breathing) and had been nursed sitting up, quantities of air could quite easily have been sucked into a large vein in the neck, like the left subclavian vessel. This would have been exaggerated by the gasping inspirations of the trooper, who drew more air at each intake into his chest. The air having formed an obstructing mass of bloody foam in the cardiac chambers, cardiac arrest would have ensued, leading to his death.

Staff Surgeon Charles Collier was a hospital mate in 1805, then assistant surgeon to the 13th Foot, surgeon to the 60th and 70th by exchange. In 1812, he went onto the staff and eventually became Deputy Inspector General. He was an experienced surgeon having served in the West Indies and for over two years in the Peninsula. He was a staff surgeon during the Waterloo campaign.

This patient was being cared for in the Elizabeth Hospital (Caserne) in Brussels.

The 1st Royal Dragoons were part of the Union Brigade of cavalry. They fielded 395 sabres and took heavy casualties. Alexander was probably hit by case shot while charging d'Erlon's Corps, or perhaps later.

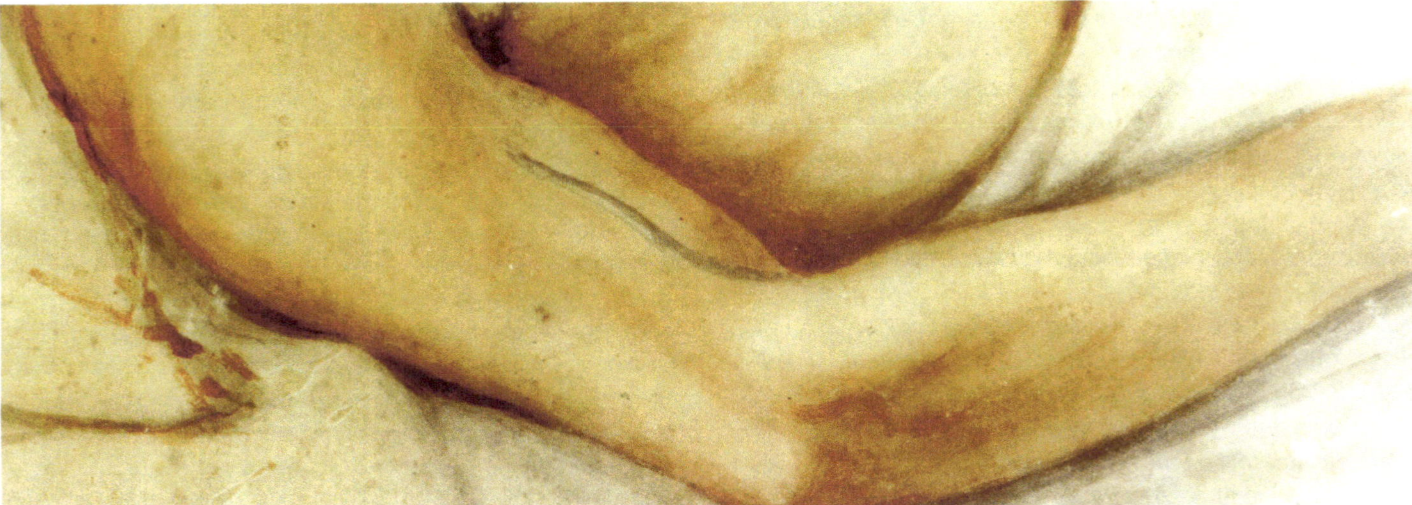

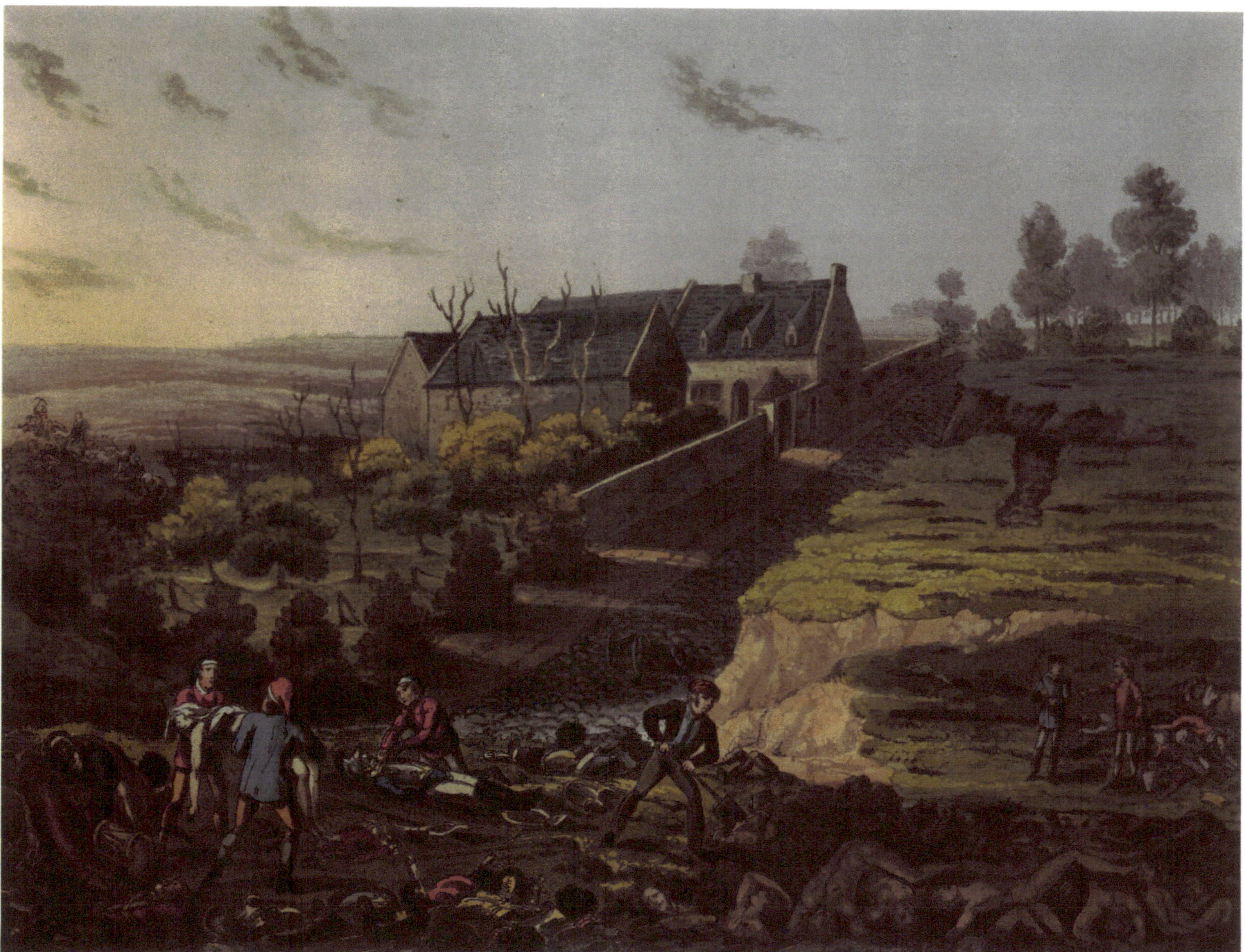

Fig.27 'A front view of the farm of La Haye Sainte. It was here that the second desperate attack was made by the French, in which the celebrated charge of Sir Ponsonby's heavy brigade did so much execution. Sir W. Ponsonby himself fell during the conflict, but the enemy were finally repulsed with the loss of two eagles, besides a great number of prisoners.' W. Mudford, *An Historical Account of the Campaign in the Netherlands.*

8. (Chest) Albrecht Heifer, King's German Legion

Notes and Case History

'Caserne St Elizabeth no.13 sec. D. The flesh of the right breast thus torn off by a cannon shot. The ribs not broken. No symptoms of much internal inflammation, but breathing with difficulty. Is this from lesion of muscles of respiration? I believe not, but from effusion.' 'Collier'.

Mr Collier alludes to this case in both his letters; in the second, dated the 20th August, 1815, he writes, 'Heifer who had his breast struck by a round shot is convalescent.'

Commentary

Very few men having suffered chest injury by round shot would have survived. This injury was the result of a tangential strike which had torn off skin fat and some muscle from the chest wall. Although it is stated that there were no ribs fractured, it is quite likely that several of them were damaged. The artist has accurately portrayed the wound with iron/powder staining around the edge of the injury.

The force of the ball gave Heifer an enormous punch in the chest and there has been bleeding from the rupture of smaller blood vessels in the delicate lung parenchyma (tissue). This creates an area of lung which is suffused with blood but not with air. It thus reduces the effective lung volume for gas exchange. It would be very painful to breathe with this injury, which also predisposes to atalectasis (collapse of the spongy lung tissue due to non-aeration and poor expansion) in addition to the bruising.

There could be other reasons for the patient's difficulty in breathing. An unrecognised rib fracture could have punctured the tissue of the right lung, causing an air leak into the chest (pneumothorax). Another possibility was Adult Respiratory Distress Syndrome (ARDS), a severe lung response to infection and other insults. As there were no signs of 'internal inflammation' this diagnosis was unlikely. It could merely be intrapulmonary haematoma (bruising).

Unless the difficulty with respiration was severe and deteriorating, no action would be taken. The course of treatment would have been bleeding, purgation and, in extremis, chest puncture of the affected side using a trocar and canula (a bronchotomy set) to release air (from a lung leak) or blood from the chest.

Like Wanstell and Alexander, this soldier was an in-patient at the Elizabeth Hospital. He was also under the charge of Charles Collier.

The King's German Legion, effectively the Hanoverian army in exile, forged their reputation as an integral part of Wellington's army in the peninsula. During this campaign, their cavalry, recognised as the finest on either side, earned the specific battle honours of Barossa, El Bodon and Garcia Hernandez, and the light battalions, Venta del Pozo. At Waterloo, they provided experience, reliability and loyalty to an allied army of 'patchy' quality. They supplied five artillery batteries and four cavalry regiments, which were dispersed along the allied ridge, two infantry brigades of four battalions' strength. The first was positioned to assist the defence of Hougoumont, and the second providing support for La Haye Sainte, where six companies of the second light battalion were the gallant defenders. The King's German Legion contributed over 7,000 men at Waterloo and their casualty figures of approximately 1,700 demonstrate the depth of their involvement.

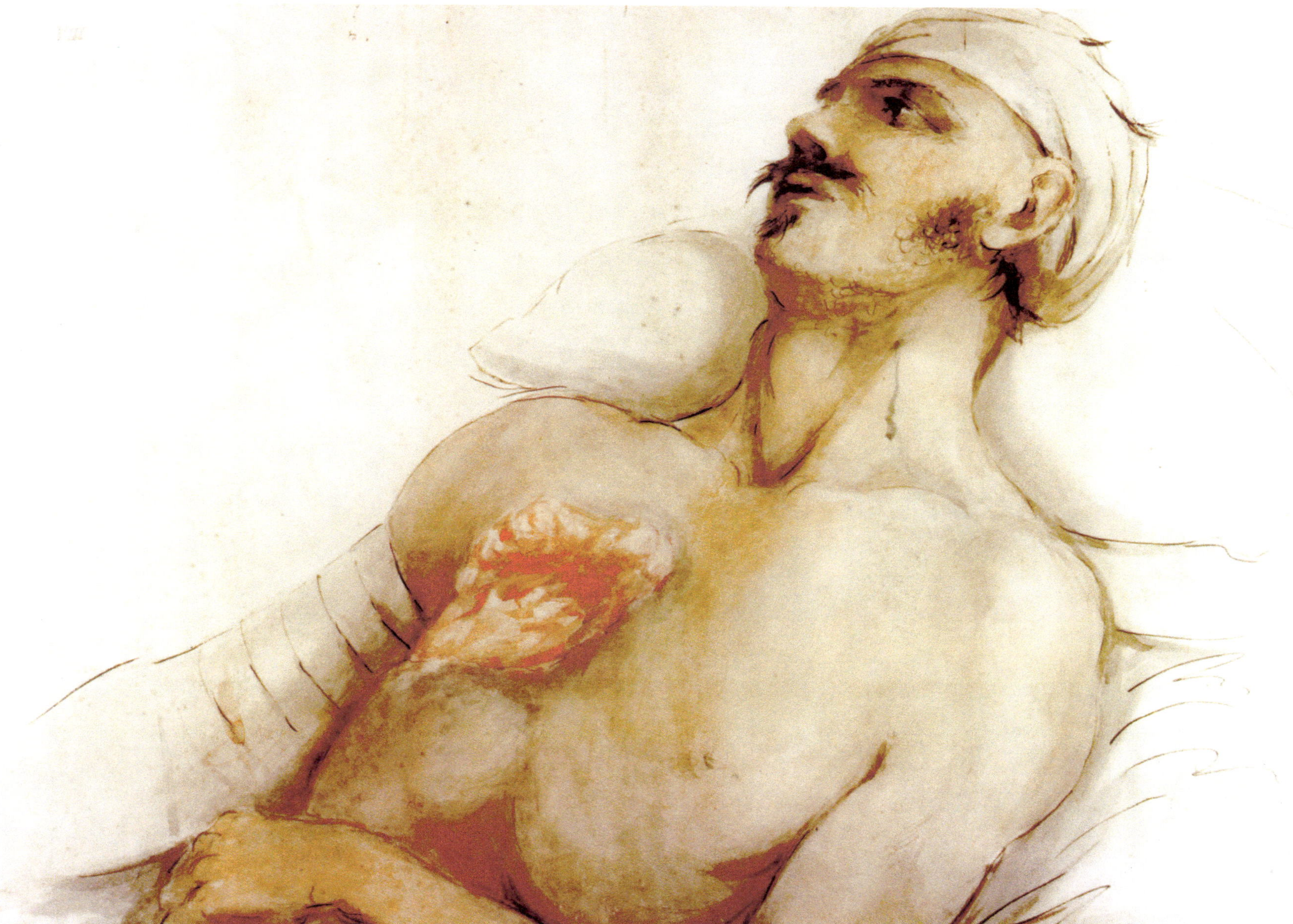

Fig.28 (Chest) Albrecht Heifer, King's German Legion

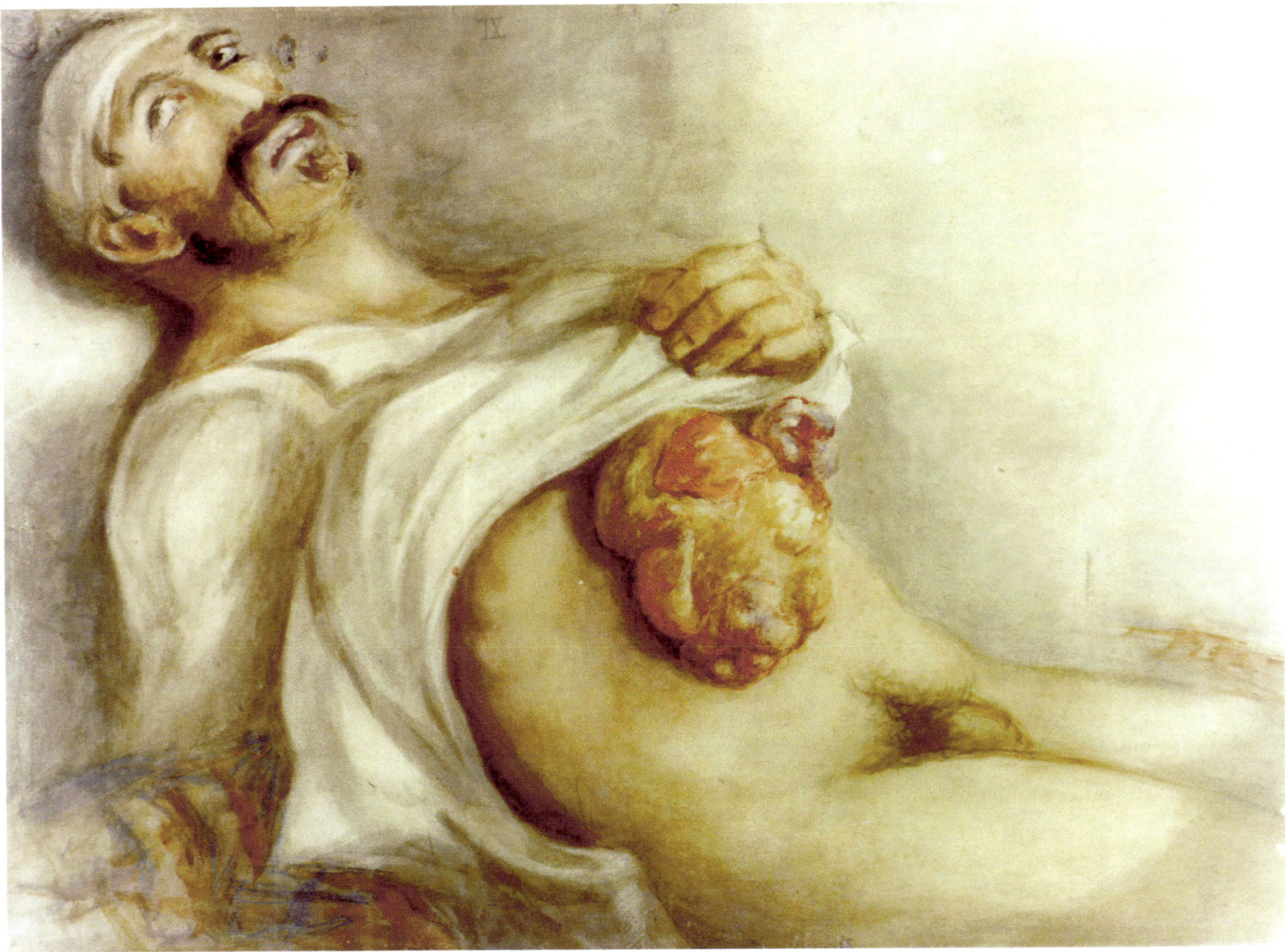

Fig.29 (Abdomen) Peltier, 3rd French Lancers

9. (Abdomen) Peltier, 3rd French Lancers

Notes and Case History

Sabre wound. The colon protruded, and completely divided; its ends retracted from each other; omentum and mesocolon also protruded. The following account of this case occurs in the sketch-book:

'Peltier, 3rd French Lancers. Belgian hospital. 2nd July. Belly opened by a sabre. Immediately the bowels protruded. Before he was off the field he had two stools, and none since downwards. When brought into the hospital the third day after the battle, the mass was gangrenous (Dr Kluyskens). A large portion of the mass comprehending the colon came away after he had made two openings.'

Letters and lines indicate in the sketch (not illustrated) the following parts of the protruded mass: – 'A, superior orifice' (opening of distal part of colon); 'B, superior orifice' (proximal part of colon); C (pointing to the chief central part of the mass), 'omentum covered with slough and slime;' D and E, (pointing to red, smooth, membranous portion on the front of the mass), 'the other two red portions are portions of the gut which has sloughed away from A to B.'

'This is the patient before alluded to, whose spirits are contrasted with those of "that pale Dutchman".'

'There does not appear to be any further notice of this patient; but Mr Shaw mentions that, at lecture, Charles Bell was wont to speak of the case as one in which recovery had either taken place, or might take place.'

Commentary

It is rarely possible to find bowel injury illustrated in contemporary texts. Their management was difficult. Penetrating abdominal wounds were not often successfully treated due to the lack of anaesthesia, wide exposure of the abdominal cavity with decent muscle relaxation and essential supporting therapy, such as intravenous fluids and antibiotics. This made surgery on the abdominal viscera nigh impossible.

Peltier was engaged with cavalry during an assault at Waterloo. He had the misfortune to be sabred by an enemy trooper in the upper abdomen. The sword thrust cut into the abdominal cavity. It was not a large entry wound. As the sword struck, Peltier would have tensed his abdominal muscles by grunting and straining. This forced out the some of the viscera, thus partially 'disembowelling' the patient. In this case the transverse colon and some of the greater omentum was extruded. This would not have been a problem providing the gut was not injured. The portion of bowel could be returned into the abdominal cavity. Unfortunately, both of these issues proved to be problematic for Peltier. First, the gut was damaged and second, the delay in reaching help, particularly for cavalry wounded (often a good distance from their unit surgeon), allowed the extruded tissues and/or bowel to swell, which further impaired their replacement within the abdomen.

In straightforward cases, the surgeon would generally sit the patient upright to help relax the patient's abdominal musculature. He would then moisten his hands (sometimes with milk or oil!) and try to coax the viscera back inside. This was often difficult because of the gaseous distension of the gut. Although puncture of the bowel was performed to alleviate this problem, generally the advice was to milk the gas along the gut, back inside the peritoneal cavity.

Accessible bowel with a simple tear or incised wound might be sutured, but when the damage (as in this case) was severe, the wounded bowel ends had to be stitched onto the abdominal wall to prevent their retraction back into the abdomen.

Peltier had a portion of dead colon as a result of injury to its blood supply. Dr Kluyskens removed the dead bowel and would have done his best to return the healthy tissues inside. The two ends of the colon would be approximated, much like the end of a side-by-side shotgun muzzle and stitched to the abdominal skin. This prevented peritonitis.

The major post-operative problem would have been the management of the 'stoma' known then as an 'artificial anus.' Socially, if Peltier survived, this would be very difficult for him. There were no stoma appliances and the bowel ends were merely covered and changed as required. This resulted in severe skin excoriation.

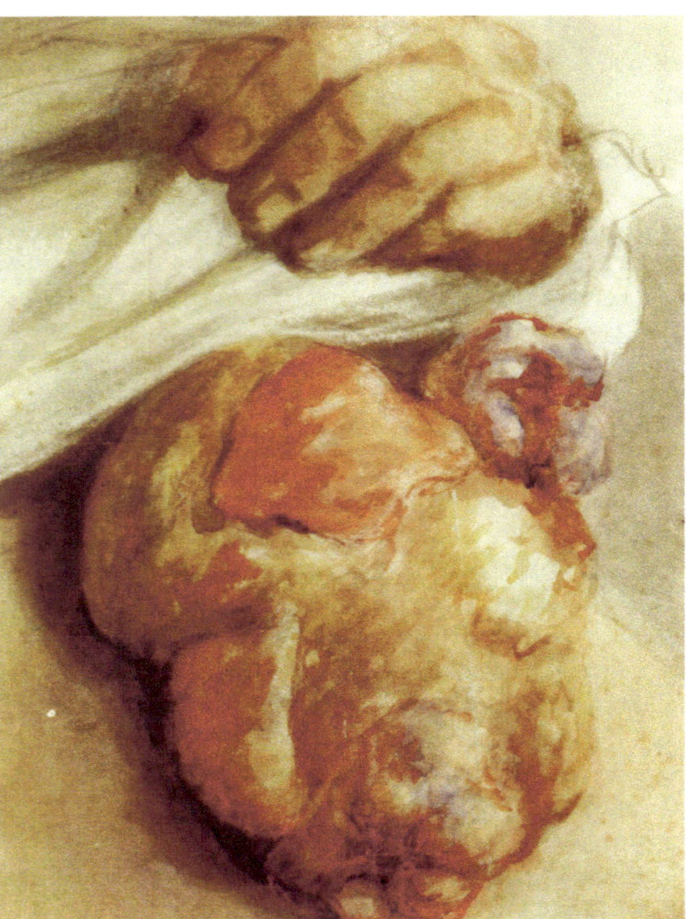

Although Bell has drawn Peltier looking somewhat miserable and gazing upwards in supplication, he comments that he was '...the patient before alluded to, whose spirits are contrasted with those of "that pale Dutchman".'

Peltier was being nursed in a civilian hospital in Brussels. Dr Kluyskens was a notable local doctor and is not infrequently referred to in Belgian texts.

The 3rd French Lancers were, along with the 4th Regiment, part of a mixed cavalry unit, and including the 7th Hussars and 3rd Chasseurs à Cheval, made up the 1st Cavalry Division. The division was commanded by General Baron Charles Jacquinot. The 3rd presented 406 lancers on the day of the Battle of Waterloo. Interestingly, this was the unit that attacked the blown and exhausted Union Brigade after its magnificent and memorable charge against d'Erlon's Corps at Waterloo. The officer losses at Waterloo were one killed and seven wounded.

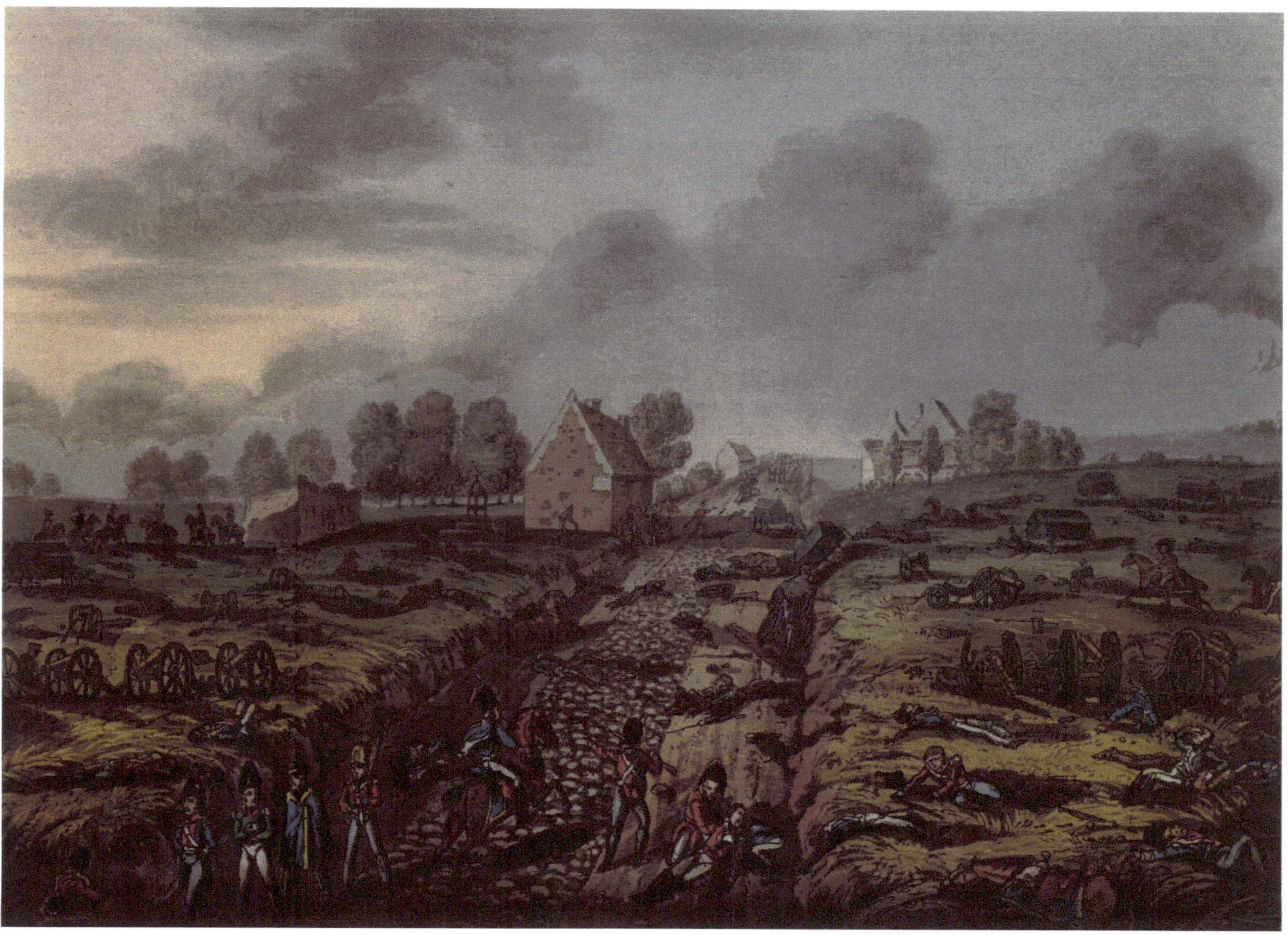

Fig.30 'La Belle Alliance, the centre of the French position.' W. Mudford, *An Historical Account of the Campaign in the Netherlands.*

10. (Upper extremity) Gunshot wound of the left shoulder (anonymous soldier)

Case Study and Notes

'The head of the humerus, and acromion process of the scapula shattered. Excision of the head of the humerus attempted, but desisted from when the injury to the acromion was found, and amputation at the joint performed.'

The drawing in the sketch-book not only shows the wounds of entrance and exit of the ball, but has the lines of the incision for the amputation marked in dotted lines (not shown here). There is also a pen and ink sketch, in profile, of this patient, in this diary at the end of the interleaved note-book before described, with the remark, 'Amputation of the arm at the articulation. I was forced to do this by circumstances.' And a detailed account of the steps of the operation performed.

There is also some account of this case, illustrated with an engraving, Plate V1, in Sir Charles Bell's work entitled Surgical Observations, *p. 231, under the head, 'Observations on amputation at the shoulder joint, and on excision of the head of the humerus in cases of gunshot fractures.'*

Commentary

Since no X-rays existed at the time, the extent of the damage to the shoulder joint could only be assessed when the surgeon inserted his finger into the entry wound. As often as not with this sort of injury, a disrupted joint was felt and this mandated removal of the limb at the joint (i.e. disarticulation of the shoulder).

The patient would generally be sitting up for surgery and supported in the likely event of syncope (faint). A large flap of skin, fat and muscle was fashioned on the outer aspect of the shoulder and turned upwards. The surgeon then cut into the joint and dislocated the head of the humerus outwards from its socket. The neurovascular bundle was pinched by the assistant and the soft tissues remaining were divided. The axillary artery was then ligated with silk or waxed linen and the nerves were divided as high as possible. The excision thus completed, the flap was swung down into the defect on the wall of the armpit, and stitched or bought together with strips of adhesive tape. The mortality in this operation would be approximately 20 to 30 per cent. Baron Dominique-Jean Larrey, surgeon to the French Imperial Guard, performed eleven of these procedures at the Battle of Borodino in 1812. Not one man died due to surgery but two succumbed from dysentery. One of the soldiers (a senior line officer), having undergone his disarticulation, immediately mounted his horse (which he subsequently lost) and, sponging his own dressings daily, he made his own way back to France. He placed a sheepskin over his wound and was healed in three months.

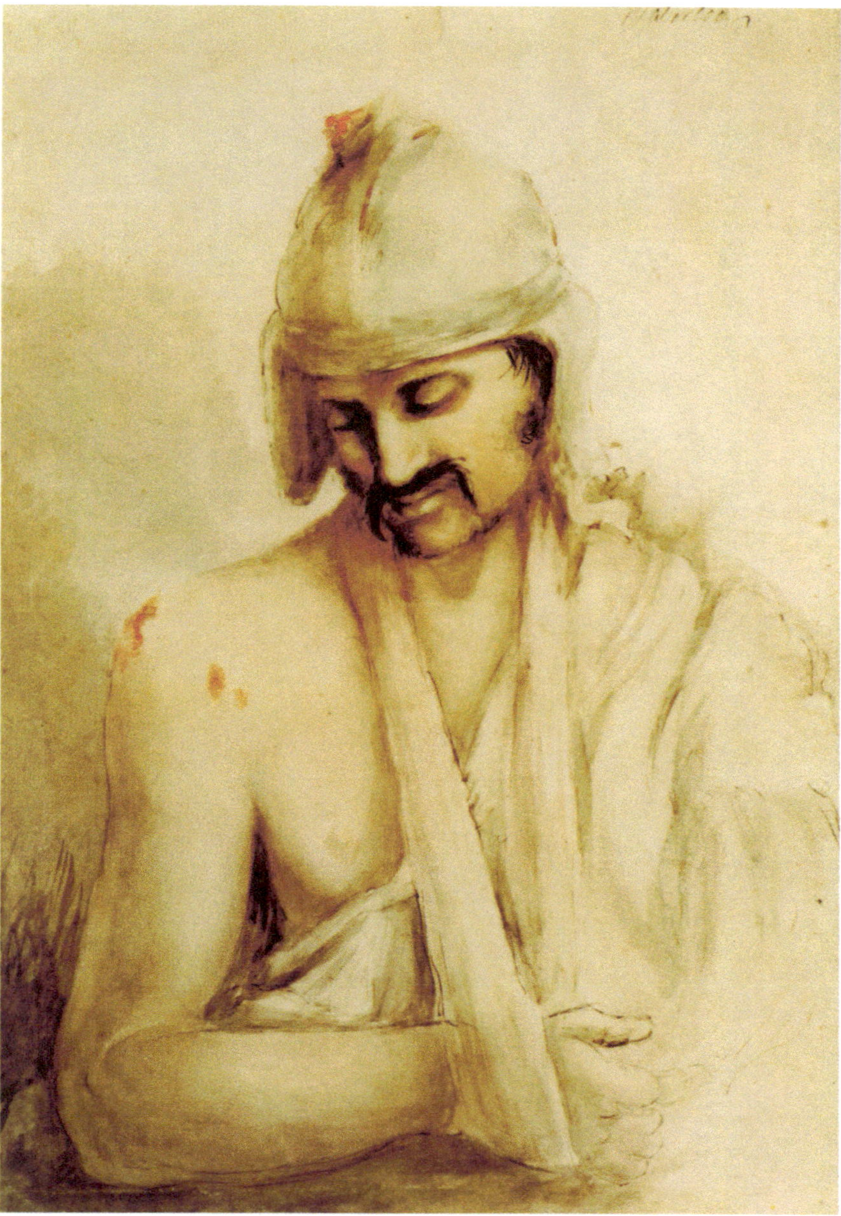

Fig.31 (Upper extremity) Gunshot wound of the left shoulder (anonymous soldier)

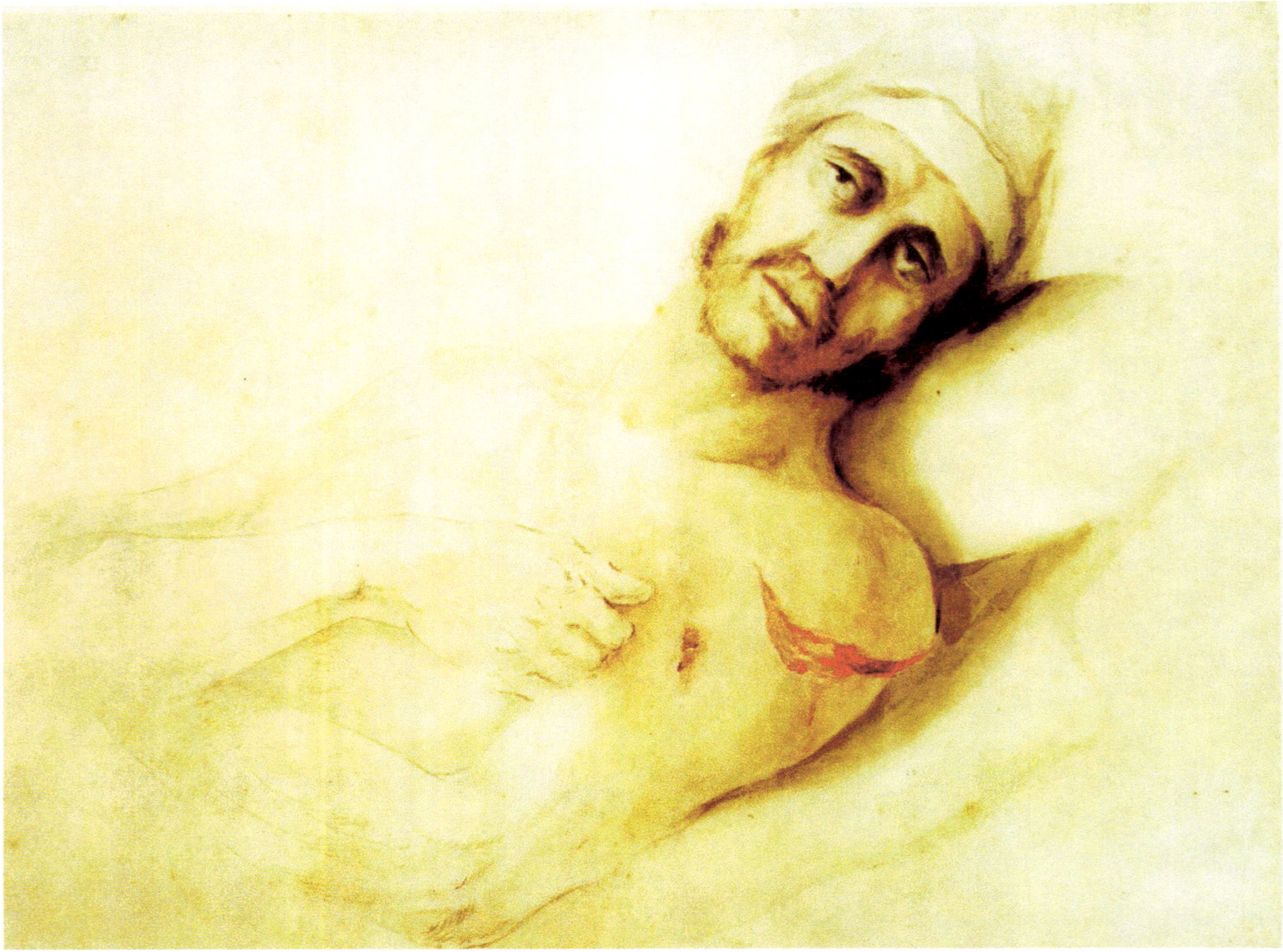

Fig.32 (Upper extremity) James Ellard, private, 18th Hussars, aet. 32

11. (Upper extremity) James Ellard, private, 18th Hussars aet. 32

Notes and Case History

Head of humerus shattered by gun-shot at Waterloo. Head of bone excised by transverse incision.

The original sketch from which this drawing was made is on paper, and has been wafered on to one of the pages of the sketch-book. It was not done at Brussels, but at the York Hospital, Chelsea after the excision had been performed. These are the following marginal notes:

'James Ellard, private, 18th Hussars, aet 32. A musket ball entered above the insertion of the pectoral muscle, passed through the head of the humerus, and went out behind. Few small pieces of bone were extracted a few days after at Brussels. On the 13th Sept. received into York Hospital, Chelsea. Operated on by Mr Morell, on the 13th Sept.' The drawing appears to have been made on the fifth or sixth day after the operation. The shoulder appears swollen, red and inflamed; and a transverse wound represents the line of incision made in the operation, which Sir C. Bell considered ought to have been longitudinal. A straight pencil line in the original sketch points to a swelling near the situation of the insertion of the pectoralis major, and 'here abscess forming' is noted. The remaining notes are '1st day, little fever; 2. feverish; 3 hectic flush; an attack of ague. 2nd visit the abscess discharged, contracted, healed. Three weeks since the operation. The man walking about the ward, with the arm little swelled or painful and the countenance good. Successful.'

This case is noted in the Surgical Observations, *p.235. Full particulars of it are also published by Deputy Inspector Morell, the operator in the 7th volume of the* Medical and Chirurgical Transactions, *p.161. See also remarks at length upon Sir C. Bell's views in this case, by Mr Guthrie, in his* Treatise on Gunshot Wounds, *3rd edit. 1827, p.496, etc…, with an engraving illustrative of the injury before amputation.*

Commentary

In this painting, the patient, James Ellard, is pictured recuperating after further surgery in the York Hospital at Chelsea, where he was repatriated after receiving first aid at Waterloo. This was a large general military hospital in England. It was built on the site of the Star and Garter Tavern, in Chelsea. There was one other principal military hospital in England, the Depot Hospital on the Isle of Wight.

The ball had passed through Ellard's shoulder and shattered the head of the humerus. The wound was initially explored with finger, probe and forceps. Some fragments of bone had been removed. When he reached Britain, sepsis had set in and an abscess had formed in the depth of the wound. This necessitated further exploration. The rather ragged transverse incision has probably been extended for improved access. Bell poignantly portrays the pain on Ellard's face. The patient's wounds healed and he made a full recovery. He very likely had a stiff or fused shoulder joint and would have compensated for this by using movement of the shoulder blade on his chest wall.

Mr William Richard Morell was a staff surgeon in 1799. Retiring on half pay in 1802, he returned a year later and stayed with the service for another fourteen years. He served in the Peninsula for four years. He worked at Chelsea, dying there in 1823, having reached the rank of Deputy Inspector of Hospitals (brevet).

George James Guthrie, nicknamed the 'English Larrey,' was a legend amongst contemporary surgeons. He was an Irishman who fought and operated his way through the Peninsular War. He was present at Waterloo, where he became the first recorded British surgeon to successfully remove a leg at the hip joint. This operation was performed on a French prisoner of war – François de Gay, on 7 July 1815. Guthrie was not just a great teacher, but also an intellect and an excellent eye surgeon. He was President of the Royal College of Surgeons of London three times, refused a knighthood and gave numerous gratuitous lectures on military surgery. His work was used as teaching material for the surgeons of the Crimean War.

Ellard rode with the 18th Hussars, an Irish unit, who on 18 June provided 396 sabres and suffered thirteen dead and seventy-four wounded, from all ranks. Combined with the 10th Hussars and 1st Hussars, King's German Legion, they formed part of Major General Hussey Vivian's 6th Cavalry Brigade. Ellard may well have been hit in Vivian's brilliant charge at the end of the day.

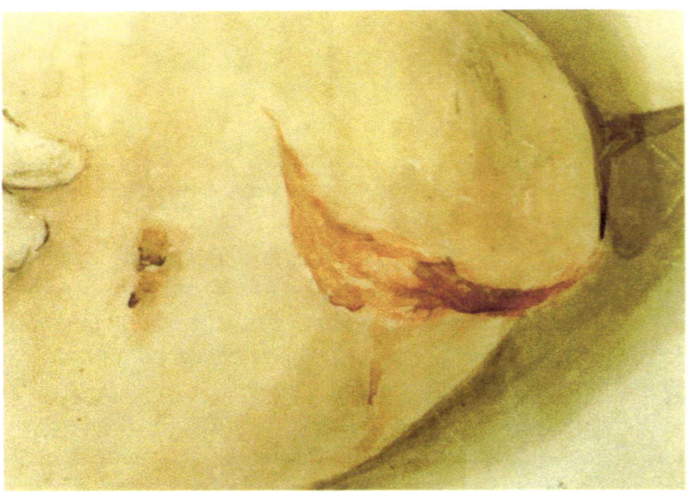

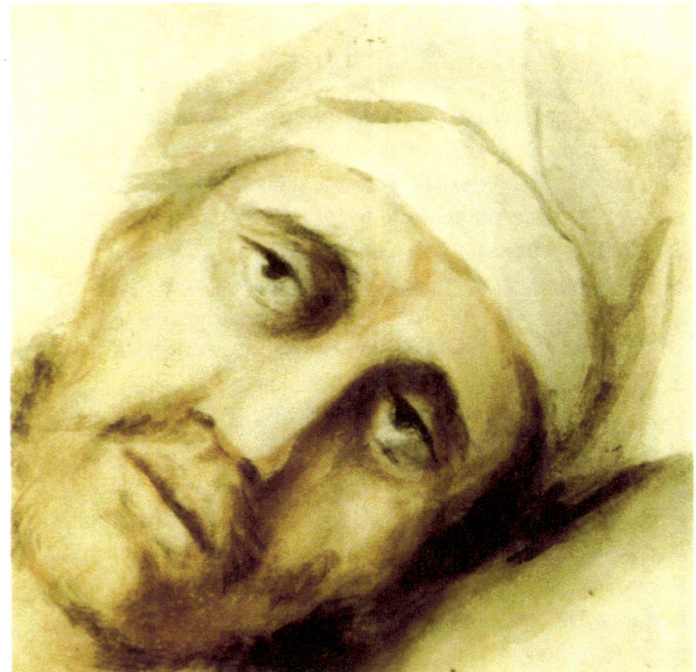

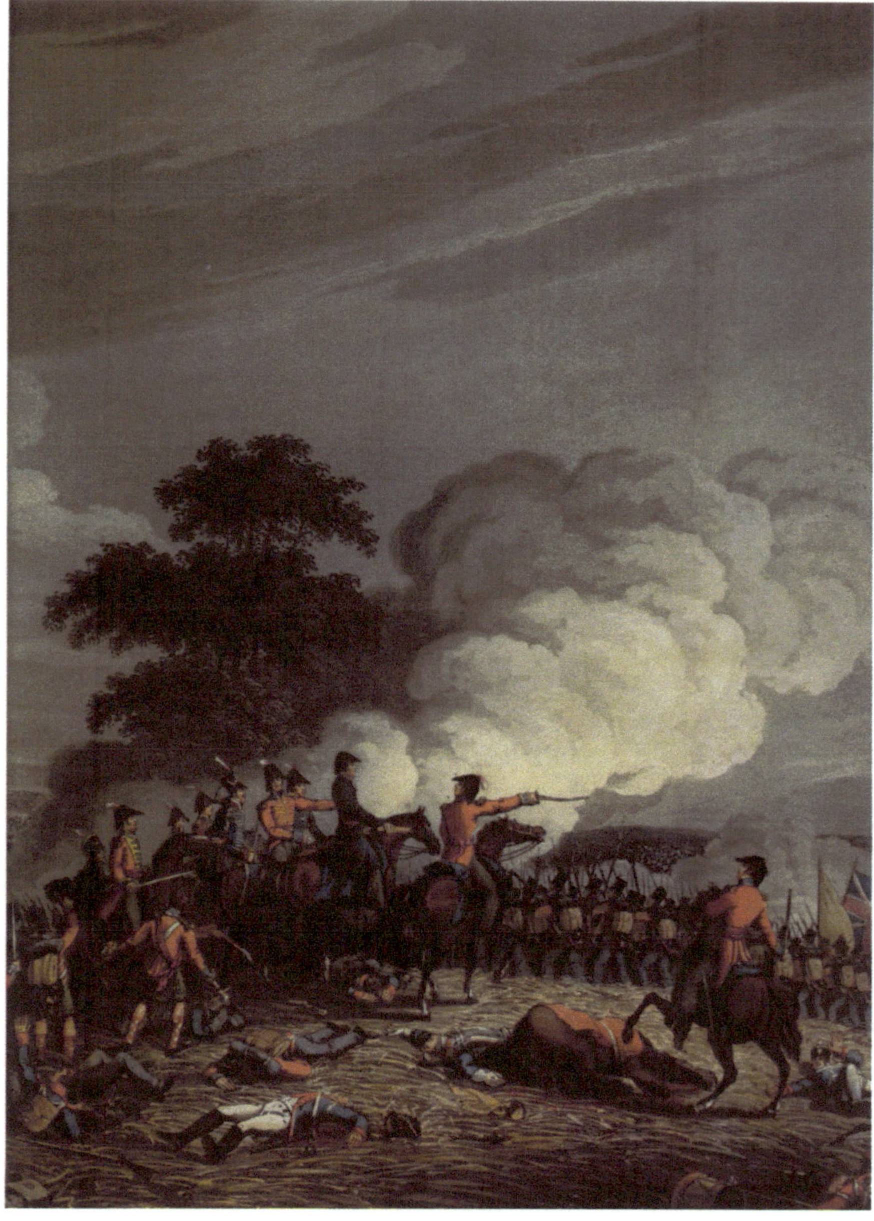

Fig.33 A section from 'View from Mont St Jean of the Battle of Waterloo, at the Commencement of the Grand Charge made on the French about 7 o'clock in the Evening of the 18th June 1815.' *Campaign of Waterloo.*

12. (Upper extremity) Anonymous soldier.

Case Notes and History

Necrosis of humerus, following fracture by gunshot at Waterloo.

The original sketch in this case is on page 43 of the sketch-book, and was made at the York Hospital on the 13th of December.

Commentary

This case study contains little information. The injury is a through-and-through musket-ball wound of the arm. As there was a compound and comminuted fracture, the wound continuously discharged pus and was painful. The continued attempt to heal by the humerus produces a shell of fragile new bone (the involucrum) and this contains fragments of dead infected bone (the sequestra). The difficulty for the surgeon lay in teasing out the jagged sequestra from the depths of the wound. The fragments of infected bone were often of larger calibre than the defects in the shell or involucrum that surrounded them. There were specially designed tough sequestrectomy forceps, made to pull out these pieces of bone.

There was sufficient space in this case for the surgeon to perform an above-elbow (secondary) amputation. This would be carried out with the patient sitting or propped up. Small soft tissue flaps would be fashioned and then retracted with a linen or leather retractor. The humerus was divided using a capital saw and the wounds approximated with adhesive tape, sutures, or both.

Often above-elbow amputees would have a wooden articulated limb made which would strap on round the shoulder. After a below-elbow amputation, the forearm stump had a solid wooden block fitted over it and held in place with leather straps. Onto this block a simple wooden peg was drilled in, over which was passed a steel ring fixed to a short knife or spoon for eating. There were private limb makers, but more elegant and functional prostheses were usually beyond the means of most men's pockets. Government supply of limb prostheses did exist but delays and inefficiency abounded.

This patient, as were many others, was evacuated home to the York Military Hospital in Chelsea, mentioned above. The York Hospital was opened in the early 1790s to accommodate casualties from Flanders. When it was built on the site of the Star and Garter Tavern, additional huts were ranged around it and it could accommodate 200 patients, rising to 500 by 1799. George James Guthrie, like many other trainees, worked there as an assistant at the age of fifteen.

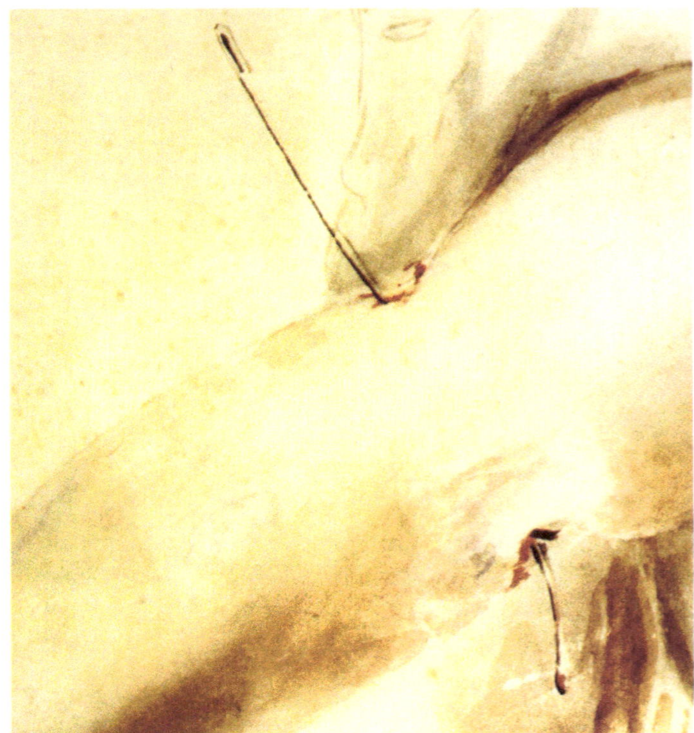

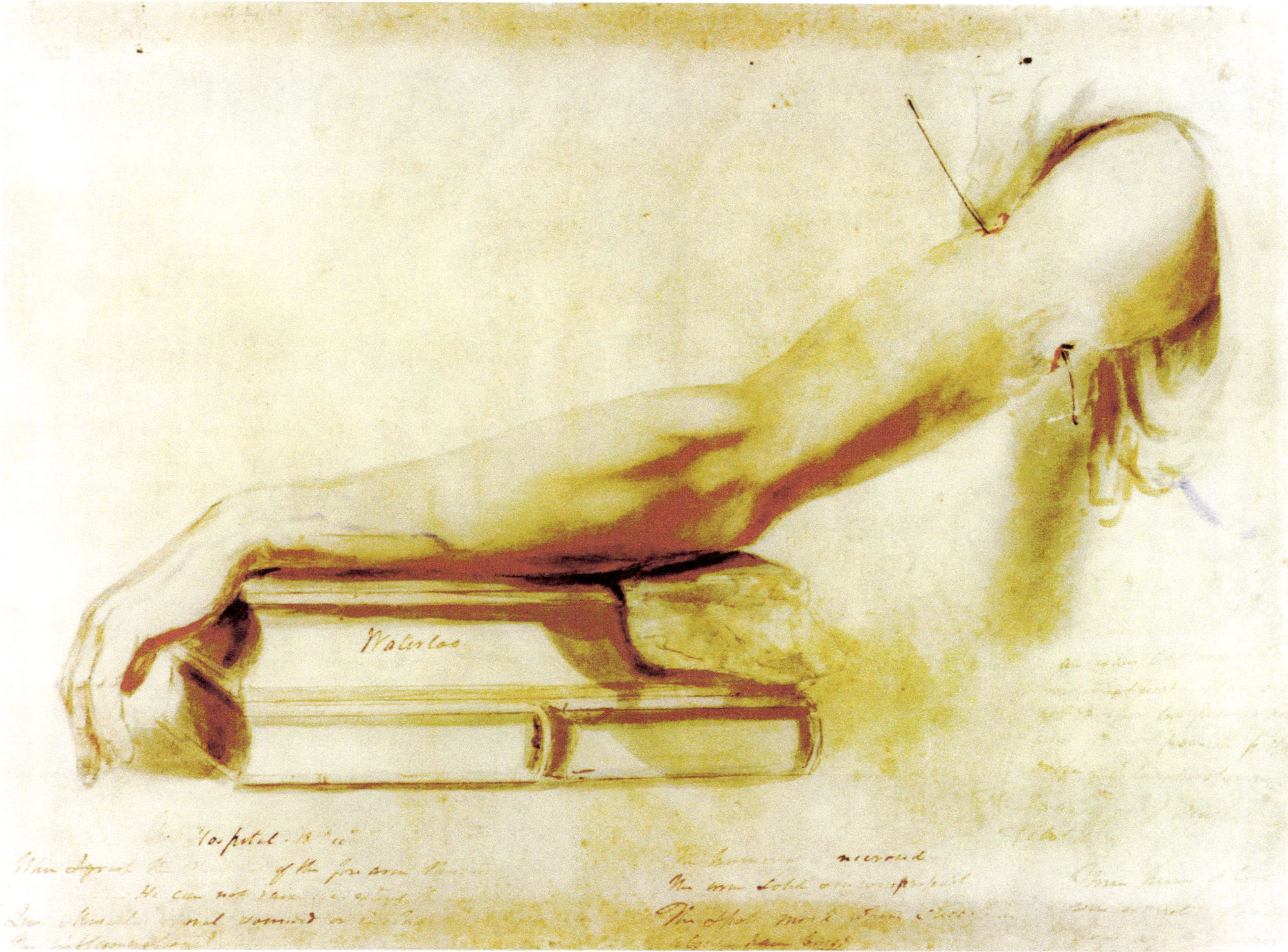

Fig.34 (Upper extremity) Anonymous soldier

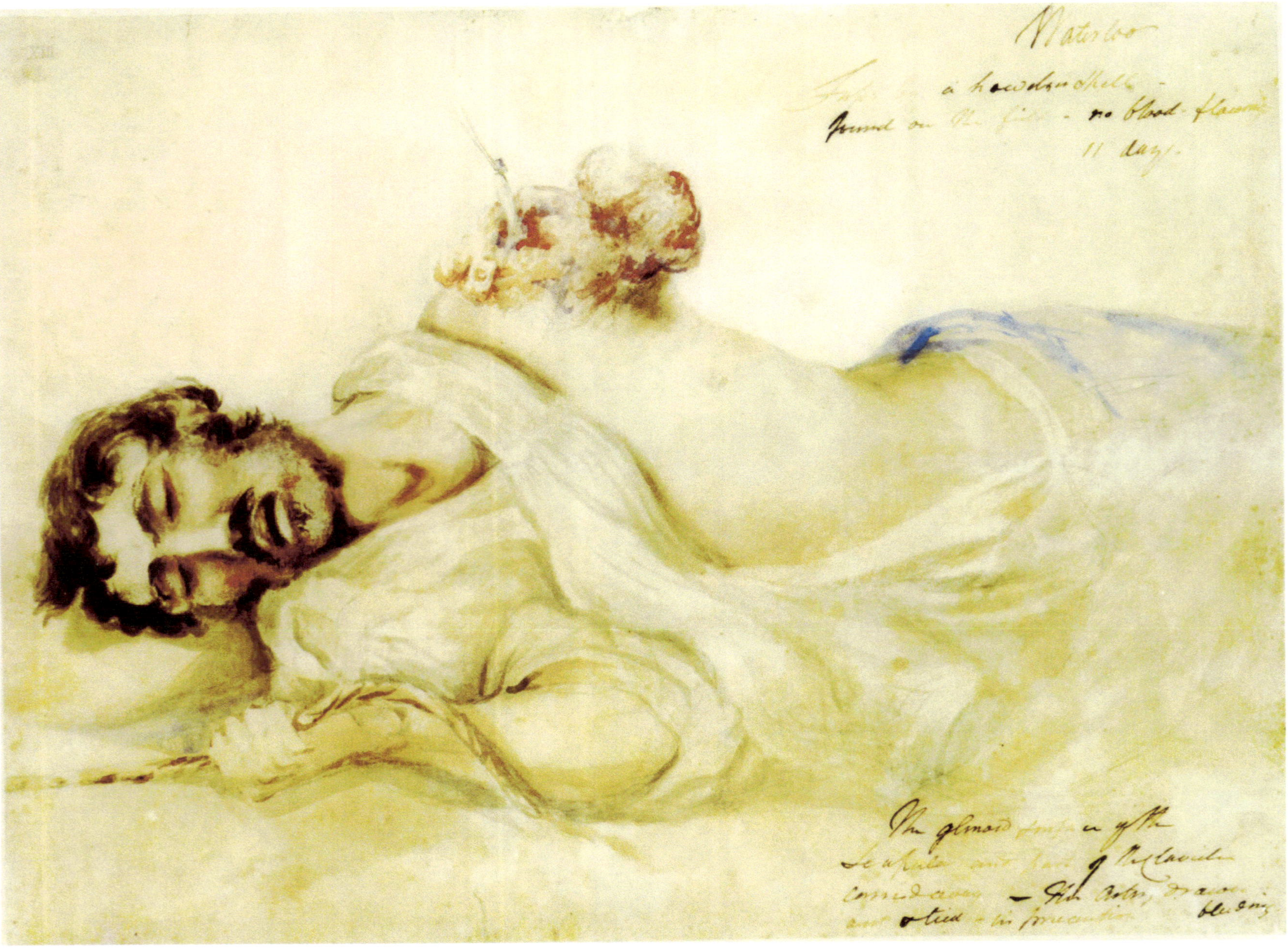

Fig.35 (Upper extremity) Anonymous soldier

13. (Upper extremity) Anonymous soldier

Case Notes and History

Left arm, with acromial end of the clavicle, and glenoid cavity of the scapula, carried off by cannon shot.

This is one of the early sketches in the sketch-book. The notes with the sketch are the following:

'On the field by howitzer shell; head of scapula, glenoid cavity, and part of clavicle. Artery taken up on the field. Eleven days and no haemorrhage. Wound healthy. This man will do well, with support and due compression of the granulations.'

In one of the letters from Brussels to Mr Bell, dated Sept. 12, 1815, and signed 'John Boggie,' the recovery of this patient is thus referred to: – 'The case which you saw in my division, of the shoulder torn off, is now nearly well. He left this [? place] *a few days ago with the invalids. The acromion process, which had been left bare, dropped off about a month ago.'*

Commentary

This soldier's left arm was torn off by a large fragment of iron from a common shell, which exploded near him. The interesting feature of this soldier's management is that the axillary artery appears to have been ligated on the field, as a first aid manoeuvre. This is clearly illustrated in Bell's picture. Many avulsion injuries such as this would, if left, stop bleeding by narrowing (vasoconstriction) of the artery as a natural response to tearing. This was a life-saving physiological event. Many other similar casualties would die, bleeding and unattended. This man was obviously near enough to a surgeon to have a ligature thrown around the vessel. The battalion assistant surgeon was the most likely person to have carried out this ligation, using his fingers and a silk or linen ligature. Initial control of haemorrhage was accomplished mostly by the use of a bandage or a simple field tourniquet.

The painting shows the patient holding on to a rope with his good arm to help him pull himself into different positions. Thus he was able to compensate for the loss of his other arm.

John Boggie wrote to Bell in September about this soldier. Boggie was a warranted hospital mate prior to being commissioned as assistant surgeon to the 28th Foot in 1801. Six years later he was surgeon to the 45th and subsequently went back to the 28th. Having served in Egypt, Copenhagen and the Peninsular for three years, he was recalled to the Staff in the spring of 1815. At Waterloo he was thirty-six years-old and later took an MD at Edinburgh at the age of thirty-eight.

The common shells of the time were shot from a French 6-inch howitzer and consisted of hollow iron spheres filled with black powder. The missile was fired with an upward trajectory and as the ball left the muzzle, its fuse was ignited. Provided it exploded before landing, airbursts produced a showering of debris. It is of course possible that the man was wounded by 'friendly fire,' e.g. a round from a British 5½-inch howitzer. There were 20 howitzers in Bonaparte's 'Grand Battery' at the battle. Interestingly, though 3,600 rounds were fired in 30 minutes from this battery, there were only approximately 500 casualties. These were, however, the most unnerving wounds, inflicted on 'cold' static troops who could not retaliate.

14. (Upper Extremity) Serjeant (sic) Anthony Tuittmeyer, 2nd Line Battalion, King's German League

Case Notes and History

'Serjeant Anthony Tuittmeyer, 2nd Batt. K.G.L. L'Hopital des Jesuites. Taken off by cannon shot. The incision through the deltoides, down to the bone; and the saw used so as to leave the head in the cavity. This, with a little picking away of the bone, will make a good operation. Staff Surgeon Hennen.'

Plate VII, in Sir C. Bell's Surgical Observations, *is an engraving from this drawing. The following description is given:*

'He belonged to the German Legion, and a round shot carried off his arm on the field of Waterloo. In this condition, unsubdued, he rode upright into Brussels, fifteen miles, and presented himself to Dr Bach at the hospital of St Elizabeth. When put into bed he fainted, and remained insensible for half an hour.'

Commentary

This is one of those almost incredible feats of stoicism by a wounded man. We are not certain as to how his bleeding was sufficiently controlled on the field to enable him to seek out a mount and ride to the St Elizabeth Hospital. He must have been given or purloined the horse for the purpose. The day was hot and it is surprising that he was not faint long before arriving at Brussels!

A small piece of humerus remained in the shoulder socket. An incision was made through the thick muscles of the upper arm/shoulder. This cut was made around the arm and allowed the capital saw to trim off the piece just below the joint, leaving the head (ball) of the humerus in the joint – a lesser procedure than a full disarticulation. The bony point at the tip of the shoulder, formed by the acromion process of the scapula (shoulder blade), overhangs the shoulder joint and had obviously been severely damaged and would eventually separate.

John Hennen was probably the operative surgeon. He was an Irish surgeon, born in Castlebar in 1779 and was deserved of great renown. He wrote an excellent book on surgical procedures, *The Principles of Military Surgery*, based on much experience and expertise gained in the Peninsular War. He was the author of another book on *Medical Topography of the Mediterranean*. He served in the 40th Foot, 3rd Dragoons, Irish Light Infantry, 7th Garrison Battalion and 30th Foot. From the autumn of 1811 he was a staff surgeon, then he was appointed Deputy Inspector of Hospitals and eventually became a brevet Inspector of Hospitals in 1823. He died young of yellow fever on garrison duties at Gibraltar in 1828. There is a memorial there to this very able military surgeon.

Christian William Bach had served with the King's German Legion (KGL) as assistant surgeon to the 2nd Light Infantry battalion from 1805. Then, having been assistant surgeon to the Cape Regiment, he became surgeon to the Duke of Brunswick's Oel's Corps in 1809. In 1813 he was appointed to the Staff (Continent only) at Waterloo and worked in the St Elizabeth Hospital, where Tuittmeyer found him. Bach died at Wurtemberg prior to 1824.

The 2nd Line Battalion, King's German Legion, served with distinction at Waterloo, being part of Sir Henry Clinton's 2nd Division. The battalion was placed on the right of Wellington's line. It fielded 527 bayonets and served in De Platt's Brigade. De Platt himself was killed in the battle as was Lieutenant J. C. Schroder, commanding the Battalion. There were 107 killed, wounded and missing from the 2nd Line on the day.

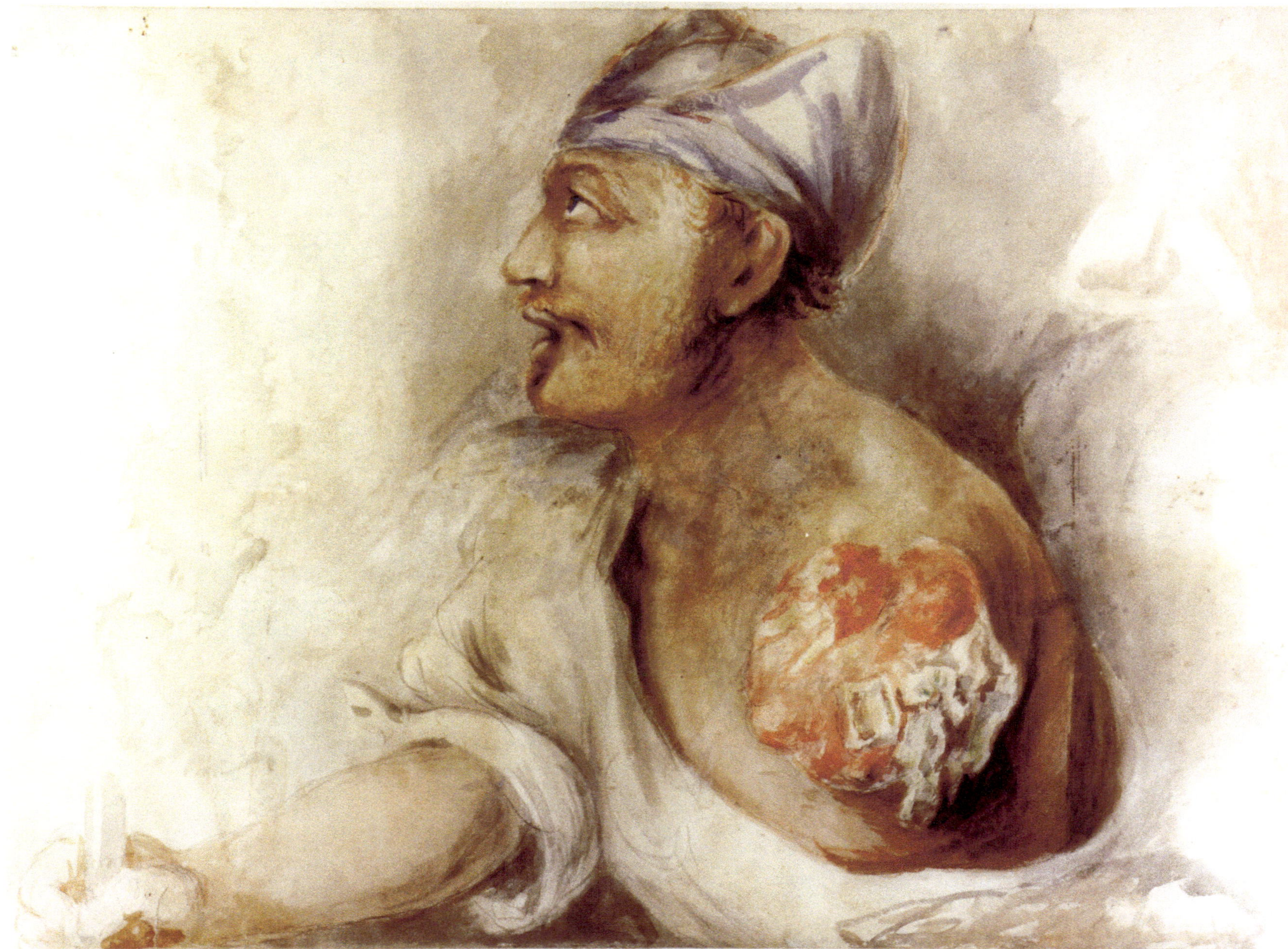

Fig.36 (Upper Extremity) Serjeant (sic) Anthony Tuittmeyer, 2nd Line Battalion, King's German Legion

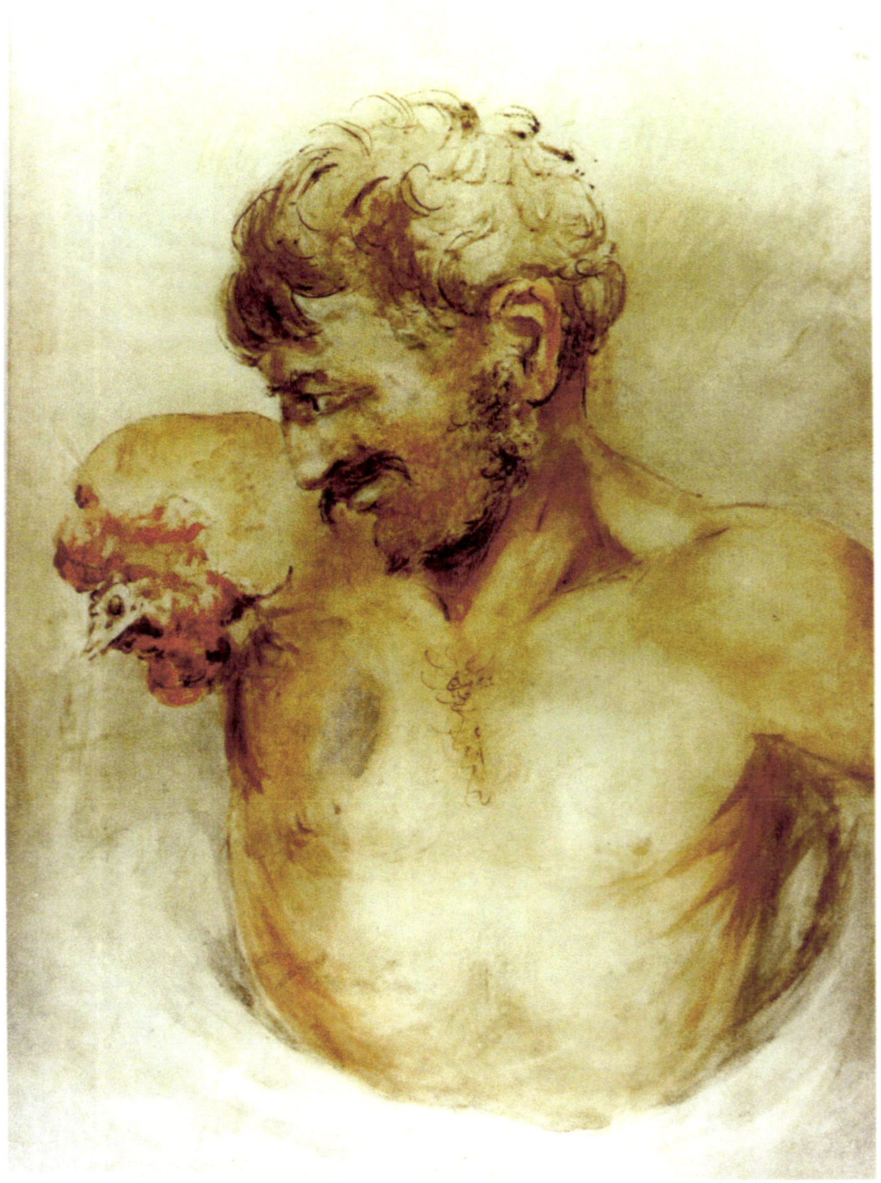

Fig.37 (Upper extremity) Anonymous trooper, Brunswick Hussars

15. (Upper extremity) Anonymous trooper, Brunswick Hussars

Case Notes and History

Right arm carried off close to the shoulder-joint by cannon shot. This drawing is very similar to the preceding one. Among the marginal notes, with the original sketch, are:

'Brunswick Hussars, 16th. A great deal of blood on the field; it stopped spontaneously This was amputated by taking the head out of the socket, and the artery tied. This very unnecessary.'

Commentary

There are few details of this case. This was an all too frequent injury – limb avulsion with round shot. The bleeding had ceased 'spontaneously.' With such a tearing injury, the main blood vessels were pulled apart and not cut clean across. Tissue chemicals were released and intense vasoconstriction of the artery then took place. Men would literally appear with the large vessel oscillating in time with the patient's pulse, but no blood leaking out! No doubt this hussar had the presence of mind to press on the stump for as long as he was able.

Bell clearly did not operate on this man. He was in fact rather critical of the case management. On the whole, surgeons of great ability but perhaps with less battle experience than others seemed to be fairly conservative. Men such as John Hunter and both John and Charles Bell were often seen to promote 'letting nature take its course' and desisted from traumatic surgical disruption which often seemed to offer little benefit.

Having said this, if the tissues were very macerated, swollen and bruised, surgical débridement (a term commonly used today to infer cleaning up a wound, see the following case) might be a life-preserving manoeuvre. I suspect that this was a very swollen and inflamed wound, and what Bell meant by his comments was that, having put this man through a further painful procedure, there was little benefit of 'completion' disarticulation.

The Brunswick Hussars were part of the Duke of Brunswick's contingent of 6,244 men which was heavily engaged at Quatre Bras, where the Duke was shot through the chest and died. Sadly, his father had been killed, shot through both eyes at the Battle of Eylan in 1807. Losses at Quatre Bras totalled 846 and at Waterloo 600, a rate of 23 per cent overall.

There were four squadrons of (the 2nd) Brunswick Hussars (684 sabres) and one squadron of Brunswick Uhlans (235 troopers) in the whole Brunswick cavalry contingent. Major von Cramm, commanding the 2nd Brunswick Hussars, was killed at Quatre Bras. Since there were more casualties at the latter conflict, it is quite likely that the soldier in this case study was hurt on the 16th, hence the annotation 16th after his unit. This number, however, could also apply to his bed or row number in a Brussels hospital.

16. (Upper extremity) Voultz, King's German Legion

Notes and Case History

Arm shattered from the elbow to the shoulder-joint. Incomplete amputation has been performed.

The patient from whom this drawing was taken made a very remarkable recovery from an attack of tetanus; and the history which is given in two of the letters in the collection is rather fully extracted, on account of the interest attached to the case, and because I have not been able to find it noticed in the writings of Hennen, Guthrie, Ballingall, S. Cooper or elsewhere. The following are the marginal notes with the original drawing in the sketch-book:

'Caserne Elizabeth, 1st July. Voultz, King's German Legion. Had his arm completely shattered from the elbow to the shoulder-joint; parts destroyed; no bleeding. On coming here, a kind of amputation was performed. Difficulty of securing the artery, by which a pint of blood was lost. The wound was in a sloughy state; now clean. Being consulted, I advised that an incision should be made in the deltoid, in the length of the remaining shattered humerus; that the dissection should be carried close to the bone; the light saw then used, to cut across the neck of the humerus, so as to leave the head of the bone in the joint. Collier. A,B,C,D, pieces of the humerus shattered, isolated, and sticking to the granulations by their outer surfaces. D is a remaining slough.' These are not shown.

Mr Collier, in his first letter, dated Brussels, August 5, 1815, thus describes the progress of the case:

'On Voultz, of the German Legion, I performed the operation we talked over, and, I add with gratification, successfully; i.e., it now offers every prospect of a speedy cure. I cannot recall whether, at the time you saw him, he had appearance of a tetanic spasm; but prior to my undertaking anything, it was so confirmed that I deemed it necessary to call a consultation; and having then our opinion confirmed of its absolute necessity for any chance of life, I carried what had been before conned over into execution. I found no difficulty in dissecting the muscles from the bone, and very little in sawing it close to the head. With two incisions I removed all those splinters of bone which appeared thickened and diseased. There was very little haemorrhage, as the axillary artery was not touched; but the head in the socket was some impediment to the meeting of the flaps, and I now regretted that this had not been taken away. The spasm appeared neither augmented nor diminished by the operation. The countenance became strongly tetanic; jaws were fixed; the least effort to swallow produced the most frightful convulsion; his tongue, caught between his teeth, was sadly ulcerated. The emprosthotonos was succeeded by opisthotonos, and of as marked a character as I have ever witnessed. When sitting on the side of his bed I have seen him thrown on his back, and the body arched by the power of the muscles; and yet through all this, and through some sloughing of the stump, which occurred, he has struggled. He is now free, for some days, from spasm, which gradually subsided after three weeks. The stump is fast closing up, and he walks about the ward, and is considered a convalescent patient.'

'P.S. There are but two cases living of all who had this affection – this man and a French officer. His death was constantly anticipated by all, and by none more than myself, on account of the general ill success of our means in these cases.'

In a second letter, dated August 20, Mr Collier writes, 'Voultz will soon be well. His health is good, and the spasm has long since yielded. The stump is nearly healed.'

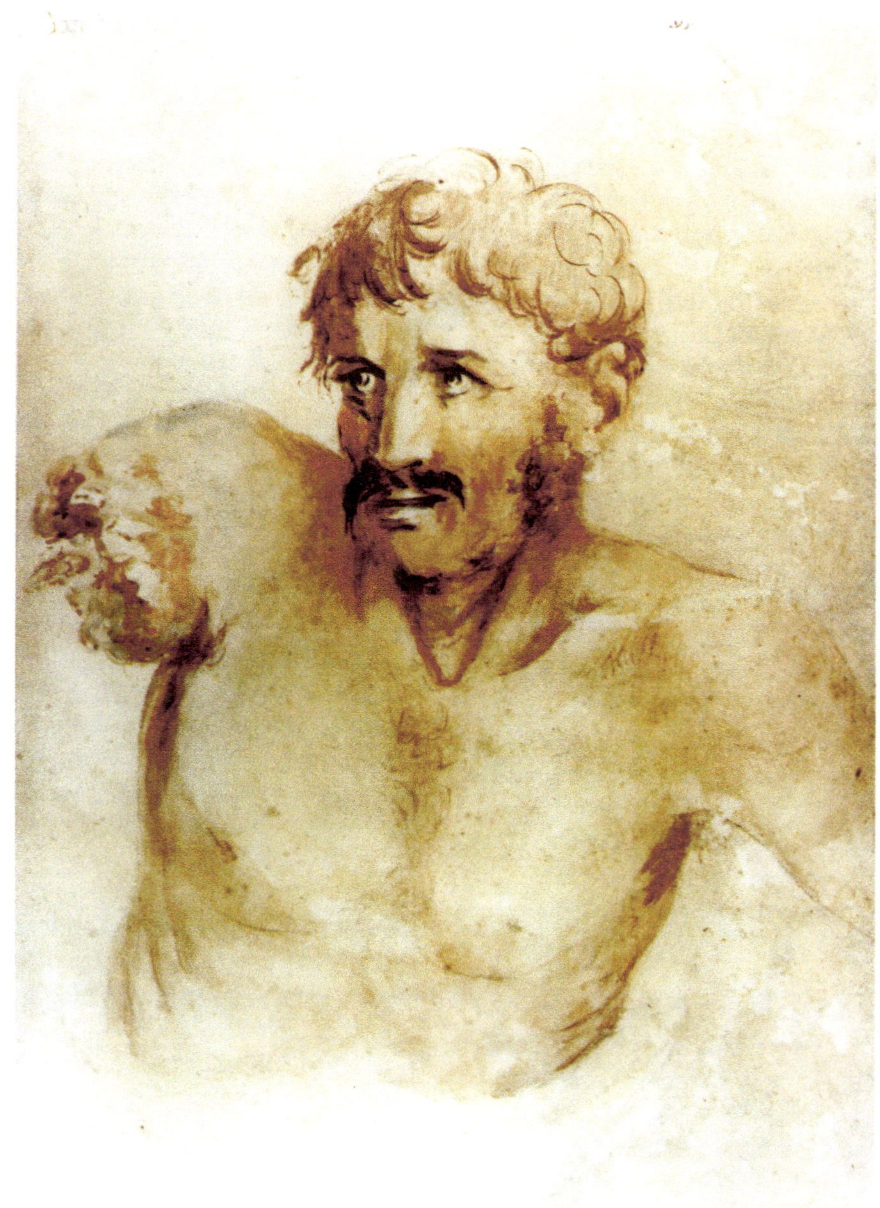

Fig.38 (Upper extremity) Voultz, King's German Legion

Commentary

This is perhaps the most interesting of all the watercolours, highlighted by the incredible fortitude of the patient and the relative rarity of survival following severe injury, surgery, sepsis and, in particular, a full attack of opisthotonic tetanus. There had obviously been a consultation between Collier and Bell and a decision was made to tidy up the wound surgically and cut the bone just below the neck of the humerus, a very high above-elbow amputation. The two incisions discussed were probably vertical and allowed the swollen soft tissues to be retracted and the humerus divided further up. He might well have used a finger saw, as space was limited.

Collier also performed some débridement of the wound. This literally means 'unbridling' and was originally a procedure performed to release tissues swollen with inflammation and injury which were compressing blood vessels. Today we call this procedure fasciotomy. Releasing such tissue tension allowed blood to flow again. The term débridement is still used and has now come to mean a thorough trimming away of all dead or dying tissues.

Collier had difficulty in approximating the skin flaps because the head of the humerus was retained in the socket of the shoulder joint. In retrospect, he regretted leaving the head of the humerus. Collier was an experienced surgeon and was clearly concerned about carrying out the operation in a man who had tetanus. He consulted with colleagues before surgery. Larrey often debated the place of ablative surgery with impending tetanus. Tetanus (lockjaw) is transmitted from the soil and in animal (usually horse) faeces. The offending bacterium is clostridium tetani. The disease starts with trismus, or spasm of the masseter (cheek) muscles. There is uncontrollable clenching of the teeth, convulsion and muscular spasms of the body. The patient's tongue is frequently badly bitten.

With opisthotonos, the whole body is thrown into severe muscle spasms and it arches back. It took very little in the way of stimulus to set off an attack. The condition is exhausting and it is difficult to feed the patient.

Emprosthotonos on the other hand means that the intense spasmodic contractions take place in flexion rather than extension. The patient forcibly curls up in a ball instead of stretching out.

During the Peninsular War, in 1812, Dr James McGrigor recorded causes of disease and deaths. Few statistics were gathered before this time. There were only four cases of tetanus in 1812. However, in 1813 and 1814 there were 23 and 24 cases respectively. Thirteen cases were recorded after the Battle of Toulouse. This represented a 1 per cent incidence in surgical admissions to hospital. None survived. This was an indication of the severe fighting in France and the improved surgical data collection in the latter two years of the war.

Several fatal cases of tetanus (including two commanding officers) occurred in the Buenos Aires expedition of 1807. The disease was almost universally mortal. Assistant surgeon Brown of the 57th claimed two successes through the use of antiphlogistic (anti-inflammatory) measures and emollient (skin-softening agents). He may well have been treating two forme-fruste (less severe) cases. There was at this time no active or passive immunisation for this infection, as there was for smallpox. Treatment was rest, low diet, when it could be eaten, camphor and opium. The latter drugs were sedatives and analgesics. Warm baths, blistering and occasionally cauterisation were employed, more so by the French Service de Santé. McGrigor advised venesection and extract of digitalis.

With so little chance of survival, Voultz was a fortunate and tough patient.

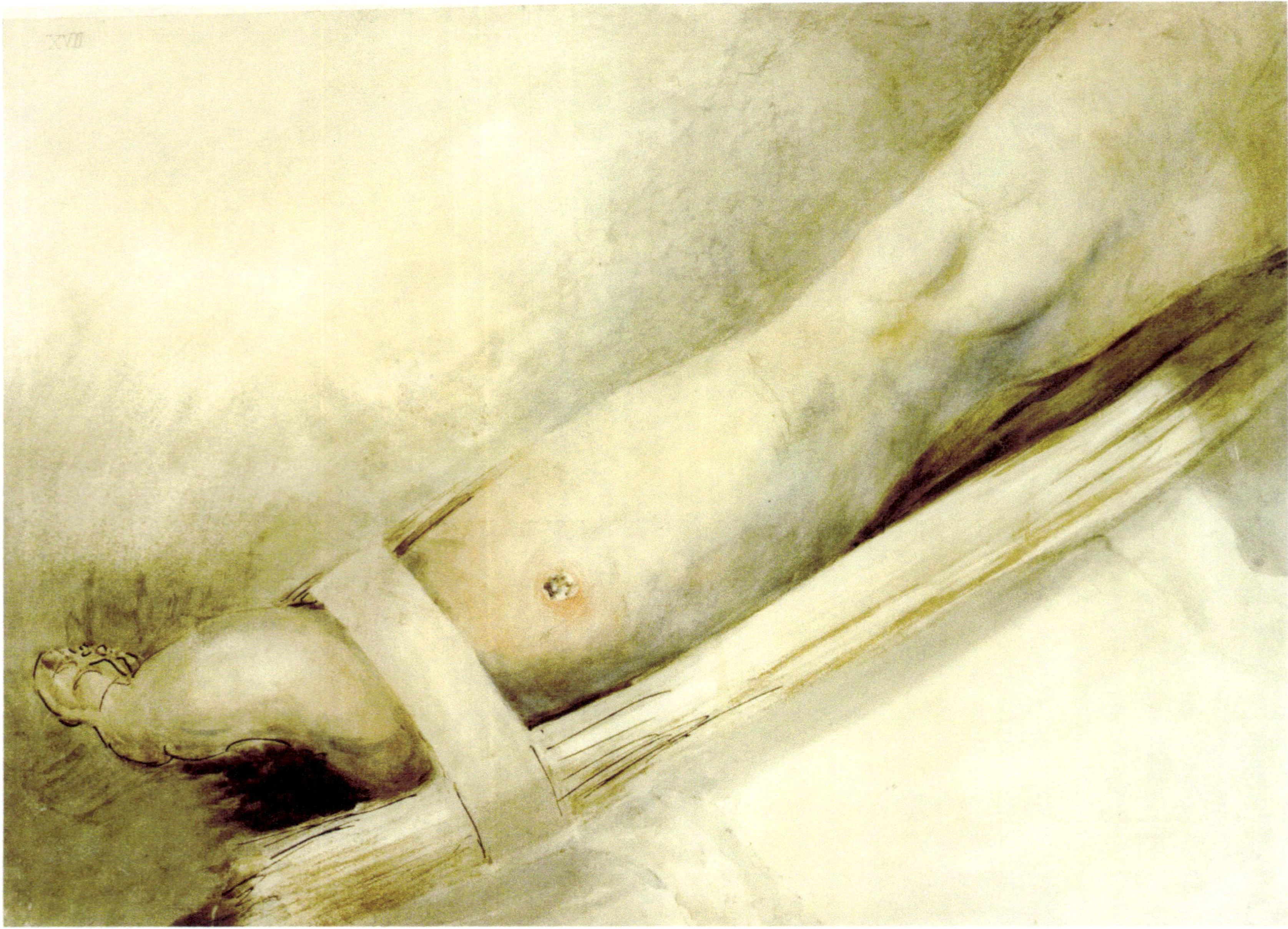

Fig.39 (Lower extremity) An anonymous Soldier

17. (Lower extremity) An anonymous Soldier

Case Notes and History

Gunshot fracture of the leg in its lower third; the bones comminuted; the orifice small; general swelling of the limb. The limb is supported by a splint made of a bundle of straw. With the original drawing in the sketch-book are the following pencil notes:

'This is an example of the state in which I found a great many limbs in the Gendarmerie, three of which I amputated this morning. On forcing my finger into the wound, it is in a sac or bag, with jagged sharp bone all around; as quantity of bad matter spouted out after the finger.' There are also references to these cases in the interleaved note-book.

Commentary

This is the only illustration of a lower-limb injury in the watercolour paintings from Waterloo. It is possible that leg wounds were so frequent that Bell concentrated on the more interesting or challenging injuries for teaching purposes.

This is an extremely instructive picture for students of Regency surgery. It told them of the difficulties of efficient fracture immobilisation. The routine provision of plaster of Paris was a long way off, forty years to be precise. Admittedly, clay, gutta percha and many other moulded limb casts were recorded as being of value, but, at this time, short wood, tin and whalebone splints were the usual materials employed to attain a degree of immobilisation for limb fractures. The service issue splints in this case have all been used up and reliance has been placed merely on a bundle of straw. Permeated by clostridia and other aerobic and anaerobic bacteria and providing only the flimsiest of supports, the treatment reflects limited supply and poor management of the rudimentary bone injuries.

The real basis of fracture management relied on Percival Potts' immobilisation practice: placing the patient and his broken limb in a position of maximal relaxation and keeping him there until the fracture ends were at least 'sticky' and early callus (immature healing bone tissue) had been formed. Occasional attempts at straightening or lengthening the broken limb (attempts to 'reduce' the fracture) were made with the patient lying on the opposite side to the injury. Accurate reduction and alignment was not easy because of pain, powerful muscle action and the inability to maintain a good position. As the healing continued, in lower-limb cases gradual weight-bearing was introduced. Since the reduction of the fracture was so poor, there was almost always shortening or a degree of angulation of the limb.

This soldier has had both the tibia and fibula broken and has a compound, comminuted, infected fracture site. The chances of survival with this injury and without surgery were as little as 10 to 30 per cent. Even if the fracture were survived, there would be serious implications for the patient's health with the general effects of sepsis, a chronic discharge and a very painful limb.

The correct management, with a 60 to 70 per cent chance of success, was to carry out a secondary amputation either just below the tibial plateau or just above knee. This, if performed by Bell's technique, was done with a straight amputation knife and the formation of circular or anterior and posterior soft-tissue flaps. The wound would be sutured or taped together and the limb bandaged firmly with a Maltese cross of cotton and linen rollers.

Postscript

Original postscript by Deputy Inspector General T. Longmore CB, Professor of Military Surgery. This commentary follows his notes on the descriptions annotated by Sir Charles Bell.

'The seventeen drawings, above described, have been protected by glass, and framed in oak frames, and are now hung upon the walls of the Pathological Museum of the Army Medical Department, at Netley. Mr Shaw's catalogue is placed at hand for reference. The sketchbook, interleaved copy of the Dissertation on Gunshot Wounds *and the letters of the surgeons who had charge of the patients referred to in these works, after Sir Charles Bell had left Brussels, are placed together in an appropriate case in the same museum.'* [Missing – the authors.]

Conclusion

What of Sir Charles as a military surgeon? Certainly, he could not hold a torch to George James Guthrie, John Hennen or Baron Dominique-Jean Larrey, well-known, 'hands-on', experienced military surgeons. On the field, surgery was different. This is not to say that Bell was not an accomplished and leading civilian surgeon of the day, but he had not spent years honing his skills on the battlefield as others had. His talents were simply different. After Waterloo, when considering British surgery, 40 out of 146 primary (early) amputations died (a 27.4 per cent mortality rate). During the three succeeding 225 (secondary) amputations, which is to say after sepsis had set in, there were 106 deaths (a 47.1 per cent mortality rate). Robert Knox, working in the Hôpital de la Gens d'Armerie, said that Bell claimed that out of 35 amputations, only five lived (86 per cent mortality), not commendable results for the day. Knox claimed, however, that Bell had only carried out 12 amputations, of which, '[o]nly one of C. Bell's lived.' If this is true, this is a mortality rate of 92 per cent! Admittedly, secondary amputation was a highly mortal problem but however sceptical Knox was of a visiting civilian surgeon, these were not impressive results. In Bell's defence, he would have been treating difficult cases. Most of the injuries he managed were between twelve and nineteen days old.

The words of Heneage Ogilvie, when writing on the training of a surgeon in 1945, ring true. 'Surgery needs its philosophers as well as its teachers and its skilled operators.'[1] It is certainly worth reminding the reader of the foresight of the University of Edinburgh in appointing John Thomson as the first Regius Professor of Military Surgery. He held this important post from 1806 until 1822 when he was replaced by George Balingall, a Napoleonic veteran. Both Thomson's and Bell's particular skills were in teaching, researching and, especially in Bell's case, illustrating.

It is a tribute that this great man is remembered for his many talents as an anatomist, surgeon, physiologist, artist and even philosopher. He laid the foundation for several reputations but may have done too much to completely master one. He was undoubtedly a surgical master but combat surgery had different demands of surgeons. George Guthrie once said 'Hunter and Bell had such great reputations that their mistakes took him [Guthrie] seven campaigns and thirty years of teaching to overcome.'[2]

What should not be forgotten was the fact that he was the 'photographer' of these wars. He left us a unique and invaluable record of the suffering and problems that were to challenge the skill of the surgeons and the stoicism of the victims of early nineteenth-century warfare.

It seems apposite to produce a modern record of these illustrations as a joint venture between the Royal Army Medical Corps and the Royal College of Surgeons of Edinburgh. In 2005, the Royal College of Surgeons of Edinburgh celebrates its 500th Anniversary – 190 years since Bell made the original Waterloo sketches.

The paintings also remain a tribute to the disproportionately large contribution of Scotland and the Army Medical Department to surgical support in these bitter wars. They also highlight the often forgotten suffering of soldiers and sailors in conflict.

In many ways the pictures hold a unique fascination, not solely due to Charles Bell's artistic skill, but also in the portrayal of symptoms and suffering, which in our opinion make these a unique and poignant reminder of the tragedies of war.

[1] H. Ogilvie. *The Education of a Surgeon* (WH Lancet, 1945) pp. 229–31.
[2] N. Cantlie, *A History of the Army Medical Department* (Edinburgh: Churchill Livingstone, 1974) p. 331.

Bibliography

Adkin, M. *The Waterloo Companion: The Complete Guide to History's Most Famous Land Battle*. London: Aurum Press, 2001.

Army Medical School Museum. Description of a series of watercolour drawings executed by the late Sir Charles Bell, illustrative of wounds received after the Battle of Waterloo. Presented by his widow to the Army Medical School, together with a sketchbook, a book of manuscript notes and some original letters.

Campaign of Waterloo, Illustrated with Engravings of Quatre Bras, La Belle Alliance, Hougoumont, La Haye Sainte, and Other Principal Scenes of Action; Including A Correct Military Plan, Together with A Grand View of the Battle on a Large Scale. To Which is Prefixed A History of the Campaign, Compiled from Official Documents and Other Authentic Sources. London: T. Bensley and Son, 1816.

Gordon-Taylor, G., and Walls E. W. *Sir Charles Bell: His Life and Times*. Edinburgh: E. & S. Livingstone Ltd, 1958.

Johnston, W., and Howell, H. *Roll of commissioned officers in the medical service of the British Army, who served on full pay within the period between the accession of George II and the formation of the Royal Army Medical Corps, 20 June 1727–23 June 1898*. Aberdeen University Press, 1917.

Mudford, W. *An Historical Account of the Campaign in the Netherlands in 1815, Under His Grace the Duke of Wellington, and Marshal Prince Blucher, Comprising the Battles of Ligny, Quatre Bras and Waterloo; With a Detailed Narrative of the Political Events Connected with those Memorable Conflicts, Down to the Surrender of Paris and the Departure of Bonaparte for St Helena*. London: Henry Coburn, 1817.

Museum of Pathology at Netley Army Medical Department. Report vol.VII, 1865, p. 596.

Oman C, (Sir). *A History of the Peninsular War: January–September 1809: From the Battle of Corunna to the End of the Talavera Campaign*. London: Greenhill Books, 1995.

Smith, D. G. *Napoleon's Regiments. Battle Histories of the Regiments of the French Army 1792–1815*. London: Greenhill Books, 2000.

Index

www.ingramcontent.com/pod-product-compliance
Lightning Source LLC
LaVergne TN
LVHW072327100826
845147LV00004B/659

* 9 7 8 1 4 7 4 5 3 8 0 9 1 *